YOU'RE ALREADY

Perfect

You Just Forgot!

YOU'RE ALREADY

Perfect

You Just Forgot!

Scarlett Rizvi & Phoenix Crosby
Illustrations by Alaina Rizvi

TURNING PAGES
PRESS

TURNING PAGES
PRESS

Published by Turning Pages Press, LLC

Copyright ©2022 Scarlett Rizvi and Phoenix Crosby

All rights reserved. No part of this publication may be reproduced, distributed or transmitted in any form or by any means, including photocopying, recording, or other electronic or mechanical methods, without the prior written permission of the publisher, except in the case of brief quotations embodied in critical reviews and certain other noncommercial uses permitted by copyright law. For permission requests, write to alreadyperfect@fromw2w.com

Book and Cover Design: Mary M. Meade
Illustrations: Alaina Rizvi

ISBN 979-8-9871169-0-6

*This book is dedicated to our readers.
You are seekers, fellow travelers, on this journey of Life.
We hope that the experiences we shared serve as a guide
and a compass as you traverse and explore the landscape
of your ever-expanding life. We are here with you, in
every page, each step of the way.*

—SCARLETT & PHOENIX

Acknowledgments

PHOENIX

I offer my deepest thanks to my parents, who gave me life and the beautiful gift of teaching me how to live my truth. I thank my children, their significant others, and my granddaughter, who have brought me so much happiness and have taught me how to love and be loved on a whole other level. I thank my husband, who has been telling me to write my book for the past ten years, who loves me unconditionally and fully, and whom I cannot imagine living without. I thank my sister who has taught me so much about healing and the power of love, and my niece who always reminds me that life is an adventure and is meant to be experienced not observed.

And I thank my friends and extended family, all of whom I consider family; your love and friendship make up the fabric of my life. I am blessed to have such a wonderful tribe of humans who understand what it means to be compassionate, loving human beings.

SCARLETT

I honor and thank my mother and siblings: I know you have always loved me with a deep well of compassion and care. To my extraordinary husband, your love and kind heart have created and held, unconditionally, the space for me to pursue my work. You are always by my side on this crazy adventure of

Life, and I am eternally grateful for your love and that we met on the Plane of Bliss. To my amazing daughter, you are my greatest teacher. Your love and friendship open my heart like no other. You inspire me to continue to grow and teach, for you and the next generation of seekers. I can never express how proud I am of who you are, and how grateful that you chose to spend your life here on earth with me by your side. And to Phoenix, without you, this book and so much of my life would not have manifested.

Contents

Acknowledgments vii
Phoenix vii
Scarlett vii

INTRODUCTION

How to Get the Most from This Book 8
Scarlett's Story 9
Phoenix's Story 14

CHAPTER 1
THE "M" WORD—MEDITATION FOR ALL!

Phoenix 21
Scarlett 26
Going Deeper and Putting *the "M" Word, Meditation*, into Practice 26

Meditation
This Is Me 29

PROCESS
4/7/8 Breathing 31

Meditation
Journey to Your Sanctuary 33

CHAPTER 2
I AM NOT MY FEELINGS

Phoenix 37

Scarlett 40

Going Deeper and Putting
I Am Not My Feelings into Practice. 40

Meditation
I AM. **43**

PROCESS
Notice the One Thinking. **45**

Meditation
Bringing Back the Wounded Self **47**

PROCESS
Creating Affirmations **50**

CHAPTER 3
RESPOND VS. REACT

Phoenix 53

Scarlett 58

Going Deeper and Putting
Respond vs. React into Practice 58

Meditation
Disconnecting the Cords to Your Painful Past **61**

PROCESS
Rewriting the Script, Rewiring the Response. **63**

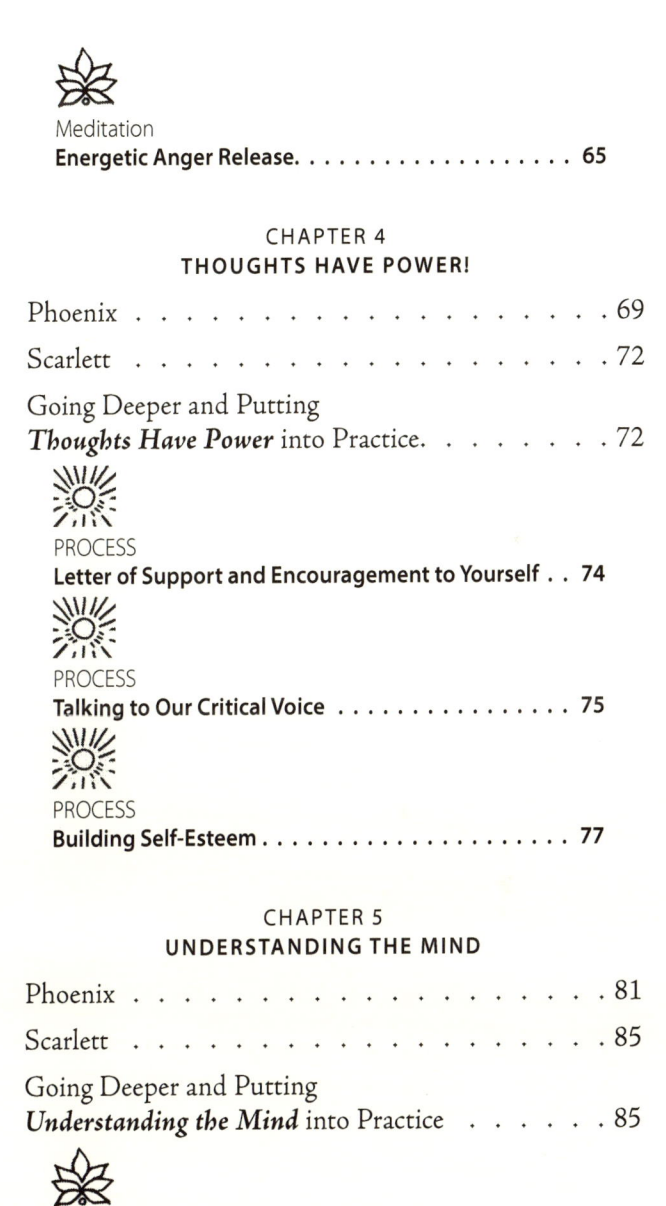

Meditation
Energetic Anger Release. 65

CHAPTER 4
THOUGHTS HAVE POWER!

Phoenix 69

Scarlett 72

Going Deeper and Putting
Thoughts Have Power into Practice. 72

PROCESS
Letter of Support and Encouragement to Yourself . . 74

PROCESS
Talking to Our Critical Voice 75

PROCESS
Building Self-Esteem. 77

CHAPTER 5
UNDERSTANDING THE MIND

Phoenix 81

Scarlett 85

Going Deeper and Putting
Understanding the Mind into Practice 85

MEDITATION
Lay Down Your Burdens 91

CHAPTER 6
THE TRUTH OF WHO YOU ARE

Phoenix 95

Scarlett 100

Going Deeper and Putting
The Truth of Who YOU Are into Practice. . . . 100

PROCESS:
Post it Note 101

MEDITATION
I AM (revisited) 105

PROCESS
CREATING A VISION BOARD 107

CHAPTER 7
HOW TO LIVE BY THIS NEW TRUTH

Phoenix 113

Scarlett 119

Going Deeper and Putting
How to Live by This New Truth into Practice . . 119

PROCESS
Bully vs. Best Friend 121

PROCESS
Releasing the Limitation 123

PROCESS
Celebrate Who You Are Right Now 123

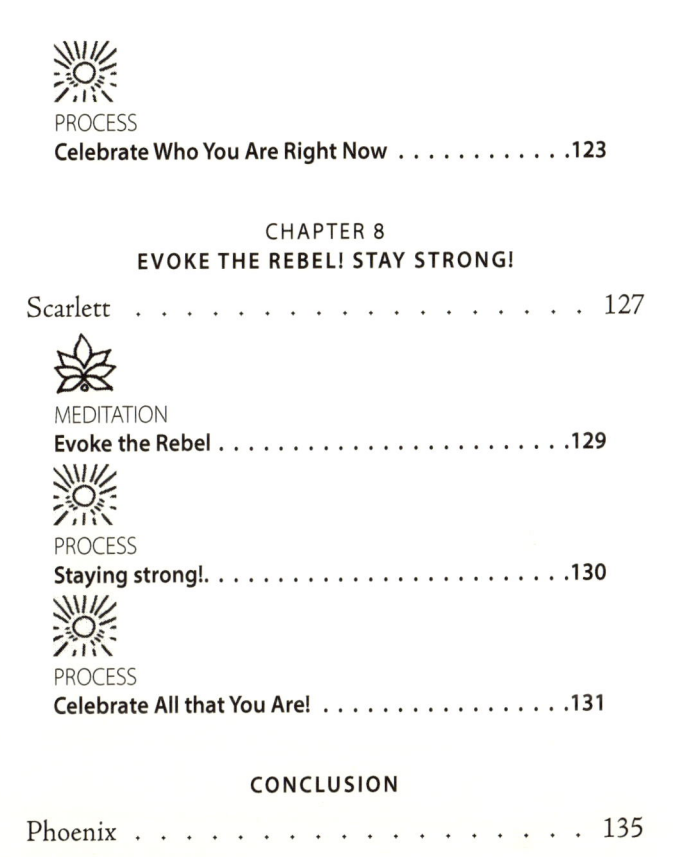

CHAPTER 8
EVOKE THE REBEL! STAY STRONG!

Scarlett 127

MEDITATION
Evoke the Rebel 129

PROCESS
Staying strong!. 130

PROCESS
Celebrate All that You Are! 131

CONCLUSION

Phoenix 135

About the Authors. 139

Introduction

I WANT TO SHARE a story with you. It is the metaphorical story which anchors this book: The Golden Buddha.

The beginning of this story takes place a few centuries ago, just before one of many Burmese invasions of Siam (now Thailand). Learning their country would soon be attacked, a group of Siamese Buddhist monks prepared to evacuate. They knew their precious golden Buddha, a giant statue, was too large to move, so they covered it with clay to keep it from being looted. During the invasion, many monks were slaughtered, and the well-kept secret of the golden Buddha remained intact.

Centuries later, a group of monks established a monastery near the large Buddha; the monks fully believed the statue was made of clay. In 1957, to make way for a new highway through Bangkok, the monks, once again, prepared to evacuate. But this time, although aggrieved and saddened by the setback, their moving plans included the giant Buddha. When the crane lifted the statue, its weight was so tremendous, that cracks broke open all along its surface. What's more, rain began to fall. The head monk, concerned about damage to the sacred Buddha, decided to lower the statue back to the ground and cover it with a large canvas tarp to protect it from the rain.

Later that evening, he checked on the Buddha, shining his flashlight under the tarp to see whether it was staying dry. When the light reached a crack, he noticed a little gleam shining back and thought it strange. As he looked, he wondered whether there might be something underneath the clay. To satisfy his curiosity, he retrieved a chisel and hammer from the monastery and gently chipped away at it. As he knocked off shards of clay, the gleam grew brighter and bigger. After many hours of labor, the monk stood face-to-face with the extraordinary solid gold Buddha.

Had the highway construction not forced the monks to evacuate, they never would have known the incredible beauty right in front of them! Because they had always thought the Buddha was made of clay, they never questioned it. It seemed obvious, so they took it for a fact. The sudden appearance of a small crack in its outer shell revealed a much different inside truth about the statue.

It is our belief that you are already "golden" and perfect … you just forgot. What does that mean? You believe certain things about yourself: You have anxiety. You have depression. You treat others badly, you don't know how to be a good parent, and so on. These things may all be true, but do not mean something is WRONG with you.

A client of mine once told me she had been to many therapists who told her what was wrong with her. They gave her a diagnosis. They told her about her flaws. After seeing me for a few weeks, she said I was the first therapist to tell her what was *RIGHT* with her—repeatedly. And with that, she said, "I need to reintroduce myself to myself."

And that is the premise of this book.

Even before we are *conceived*, before we are a zygote, our mothers and fathers have *Preconceived Notions* of who we are and who we will be. Where do these notions come from? They come from our parents' experiences and beliefs, and from the experiences and beliefs of the generations before them—from all their traumas and victories, and their stories about themselves and who they are in the world.

We come out of the womb, and judgment and labeling start immediately. We are labeled a "good baby" or a "bad baby." Our mothers are either failing miserably or doing okay. Our fathers are judging our mothers and our mothers are judging our fathers. They have expectations for us and their own child-rearing. But do they always raise us? Do they sometimes push us down so our true selves cannot rise up? If we don't fit the expectations and preconceived notions they have for us, are they watering the flower we are meant to become? Or are they trimming our leaves and taming our wildflowers to fit neatly in their perfect pots?

Now don't get me wrong. I am not blaming everything on our parents. Nor do I think they do this consciously to hurt us. As parents, we do the best we can with what we know. We try our best given our own experiences and traumas, and the stories we were told about ourselves.

We are born and we are perfect. We are 100% who we are meant to be and meant to become. Then the clay/mud starts covering our golden selves. The mud is preconceived notions about how we should be and how we should behave. The mud is religion. The mud is social media. The mud is made up of teachers and other adults letting us know whom *they* think we are and how we are doing it wrong, or right.

The mud is our peers and the mean things they say; or the nice things they say, creating an image we try to live up to. The mud is the trauma we endure. The mud grows so thick, that we forget that, beneath it, the golden self remains untouched and perfect.

The mud is anxiety, depression, self-loathing, self-doubt; our insecurities and sense of our inadequacies; our poor sense of self-worth. Once we see the mud for what it is, we can slowly start removing it, allowing the golden sunshine to break through. With each chunk we remove, the closer we are to freedom from suffering and finding our true selves.

The monks believed the giant Buddha was made of mud. They had no other thoughts about it. It is the same with us—we believe we are the mud.

That is what this book is about: learning to understand the mud—chipping away at it, bit by bit, knowing what this mud is made of, how we acquired it—so we can remove it.

HOW TO GET THE MOST FROM THIS BOOK

We wrote this book to offer you, our reader, the liberating understanding that YOU are inherently valuable, lovable, and worthy and there is nothing to change to feel good about yourself! *You Are Already Perfect, You Just Forgot* is a path out of the confining limits of what we have been told we should be—so that we may grow boldly into who we truly are.

In this book, you will learn how you can turn your struggles into strengths and pain into possibility. The processes and exercises will take you on a journey, an exploration of YOU. As you peel back the layers of who you've become, the shiny, "Golden Buddha" of your true self will emerge and you'll be astonished when you recognize you are already that confident, strong, passionate, and happy person you've been yearning to be.

We start this journey with a short, informational chapter about meditation and how to design a meditation practice that will be a good fit for *you*—even if you feel you "can't meditate" (we've all been there!). Then we go on, in the next chapter, to explain and explore how to develop and practice your own program of meditation, breathing, and affirmations. This will offer you the foundational tools to calm the mind and release the stress of feeling "not good enough." You'll learn how to create a relaxed and peaceful environment, a sacred space of your own, where—with compassion and care—you can deeply connect with your innermost self.

We guide you through the book, introducing each concept with a brief explanation of the core idea, followed by meditation and healing practices. We recommend that you take your time with each chapter, giving you the ability to integrate what you've learned and experienced. You will learn the essential, fundamental practice of mastering your thoughts, and how to create neural pathways that offer you new, empowered ways of thinking, feeling, and responding when triggered by old wounding. This will establish a robust framework for delving deeper into the healing and releasing processes that will enable you to uncover your true inner gold.

The short, informational chapters were written by Phoenix, and the meditations, healing processes, and their explanations were written by Scarlett. This format allows us to share each of our unique strengths with you. Though our writing styles vary, we are very much aligned in our beliefs and methods. So, grab your journal and pen, and let's begin this adventure together!

As an added bonus to this book, we're offering you audio versions of the meditations you'll find at the end of the chapters. Please visit our website to access the private meditation page and use the code "transformation." You'll also find exciting upcoming events such as retreats, facilitator training, master classes and book clubs with the authors. (**www.fromw2w.com**)

SCARLETT'S STORY

Have you ever felt like a stranger in your own life?

From a young age, I had a knowing that the poverty and struggle I was born into, wasn't the life I came here to live. I felt as if I was dropped off in a strange land with no map or compass to guide my way. It wasn't just the poverty, I was acutely aware of the suppression, the conditioning to give up and give in to a system that felt like it was designed to keep me small and quiet.

I was determined to push the boundaries of what I was taught and believed was possible for me. What am I doing here? What are the rules of this game called Life? How can I create my own rules? Do I even want to play this game? I felt the fire of rebellion against the conditioning and expectations of family, religion and society, and it was blazing the road in front of me.

At 11 years old, I had my inner awakening. I knew I didn't fit in this life I was born into and in a moment of anger and passion, I made a commitment, a contract with Life—"I will do whatever it takes to live my true life!"—and at that moment my path's trajectory shifted. Now I had a compass guiding me to my true north! I didn't know where this road was leading but I had woken up and my Hero's journey had begun.

Although I couldn't change my external circumstances at that age, I began intuitively to change my internal circumstances. I scrutinized my thoughts and beliefs, questioning everything. I said no before I would say yes to my thoughts. I didn't trust what I thought anymore or where the thoughts came from. This fierce commitment to finding my true life consumed me. I felt like a trapped animal in a cage, alert, waiting, and watching for opportunities that would help me on my quest.

The next few years were filled with adventures that opened my mind to what was possible. When I was 18, I married a Martial Artist and learned the way of chi and how we can cultivate and partner with the invisible energy all around us. My life was full in many ways but always there was a sense of isolation. I was a singularity. I didn't have friends or family that could relate to my internal world that kept pulling me forward. Often, I struggled and felt adrift. I questioned myself. I suffered with anxiety. I couldn't see where I was going, only that I couldn't change course. Life wouldn't allow it. I had to continue to find the courage to keep moving forward, learning and growing.

In time, my husband and I went on our separate journeys. This was the most painful experience of my life. It triggered abandonment issues from my childhood, I felt unloved and undeserving, and I believed I would be alone forever. Who could possibly love me? There were many days and nights that I found myself curled in a ball, the pain ripping into my soul. On one occasion, I was lying in bed exhausted and heard a sound I didn't recognize. It was only when I lifted my head to listen that I realized the sound was coming from me. I was wailing in pain from the intensity of my fractured soul.

The construct of my life was being torn down, the safety and comfort were being deconstructed so I could again "wake up" and build a new, bigger container for the next phase of my journey. The commitment to my guiding mantra of "I will do whatever it takes to live my true life!" was in full force again! I refused to be a victim in my own life but how do I heal my heart and soul?

This is when I found meditation. It helped me to calm the storm and find some peace. Slowly I had more and more moments of clarity and I felt the embers glowing of that familiar fire again. I was connecting with my inner self and there was a glimpse of the road opening up to me as the fog started to clear. Deepening my trust in the guidance of my compass, I continued stepping forward, one foot at a time, and to breathe. I created a mantra that I repeated hundreds of times a day to anchor me so I wouldn't sink back into the fear and panic. "I'm safe; I trust that Life is holding me and guiding me."

In time, my journey led me to southern California where I married my amazing husband and partner, and we created an adventurous life together. I studied and was initiated into the

Inca Shamanic healing tradition. Who knew this is where my life would lead me? Certainly not me. But it all made sense when I looked at my early experience with martial arts and chi. Shamanic healing is another way of partnering with the world of invisible energy. My heart and soul began to heal.

At the conclusion of my training, I traveled to Peru and learned ancient healing practices from the last of the Inca medicine people. We performed sacred ceremonies in Machu Picchu at night with only the stars to light our path. In the jungle, we *journeyed to the place of our death* with the plant medicine Ayahuasca, a natural hallucinogenic that is believed to open the mind and heal past traumas. My journey through Peru culminated in the Andes at 14,000 feet with more sacred ceremony and deep healing. Watching the sunrise over the peak of Mt. Ausangate assured me that I have never been and will never be alone in my life. As the sun rose and warmed the cold earth, the frost I was carrying in my heart also warmed and thawed. I felt alive and connected and free to love and be loved again.

Some of the most transformative life lessons I received during this journey are:

> *The pain of isolation and aloneness is an illusion, an artificial construct of the wounded self trying to create protection from more pain and hurt. Truly, we are never alone.*
>
> *Life transitions and growth don't have to be painful and dramatic when we develop trust and patience.*
>
> *There is healing and peace for the trauma and wounding we are suffering from.*

I was once told that life will teach me the lessons I need but it's up to me whether it's from a two-by-four hitting me on the head or a feather landing on my shoulder. I'm choosing to recognize the feathers and trust before the volume of Life's message gets turned up.

It's been many years since the sunrise in Peru and many more transitions have guided my life. One of my most delightful and surprising life transitions was into motherhood. At 41, I gave birth to my precious daughter. The feel of her warm cheek against mine as she lay in my arms expanded my heart and opened my soul to a depth I could never have imagined. She has become my greatest teacher and my best friend.

Our heart's capacity to open and love and share and feel is as limitless as Life itself. There is always a gift, a surprise around the corner when we learn to stop resisting and trust the trajectory of our life.

Everything I've experienced in my life has become part of my teaching and healing. As you read and experience those teachings in these next pages, I invite you to open your heart and expand your belief in what is possible for you. Trust your internal compass to guide you to *your* true north.

We'll begin by calming the internal storm that you're carrying with meditation and breathing so you can lay down your burdens and find rest. As you cultivate a peaceful mind and calmer heart you can recognize more of the feathers landing on your shoulders. Trust their guidance. There's an authentic, fulfilling life pulling you forward. Be brave, take one step at a time, and know that you are never alone on your journey. I am here with you in every page, in every word, in every breath. Life is here with you, loving you, supporting you and guiding you.

PHOENIX'S STORY

When I decided to write this book, I peeled back the veil of time and looked back at my life to explore and better understand what helped define the person I am today. The person that knows she is already perfect and is ready to share with you how you, too, can come to know this and live as *your* True Self.

And I discovered that the most formative events of my life were every day and every moment, from the most obvious to the most (seemingly) insignificant. I grew up in an upper-middle-class home with loving parents and one older sister. We had a large extended family with whom we spent a lot of time. Nobody in my family was divorced with the exception of my Great Aunt Pearl. My parents were very open-minded, and my sister and I were raised with few restrictions.

In the '70s, Werner Erhard founded EST, a Large Group Awareness Training Program, an outgrowth of the Human Potential Movement. My parents were captivated by the EST program and enrolled me in the children's training at age nine.

After my first young experience with EST, I agreed as a teenager to complete the teen training out in California the summer before high school. My childhood up to that point was a good one. The most significant event was when, at age 14, my older sister, age 16, decided traditional school and home life were not for her. My parents let her attend the Audubon Society traveling school, which meant she traveled around the United States in a bus, learning about the environment and completing her required high school lessons through her experiences, instead of sitting in a traditional classroom. While this gave my sister her freedom, it was devastating for me. All at once, I became an only child and the sole focus of my parents' attention. I am not saying this to criticize my parents: they were and are great people in my life then and today.

When I returned home to start high school, after my EST summer in California, I realized I no longer had much in common with my old friends. The girls had started to do what many middle and high school girls do: gossip about each other and act phony. At that age, most of us have no clue about who we are, and we all want very badly to "fit in" and not stand out. I, on the other hand, was a child of EST! I could see through this way of thinking and believing. So now what?? I decided to end all my friendships, except one, and start high school without friends and with the "popular girls" hating me for dropping them. At the time, this was a crisis! I mean, who does that?? Basically, I had sentenced myself to teenage social death...

Needless to say, I was miserable. I remember walking into the cafeteria, holding my tray, and looking out at the sea of tables filled with chatting chattering kids, yet no one called to me to sit with them. I felt like I was in the middle of the ocean, about to drown and all the islands I could reach were being circled by hungry sharks.

I remember crying a lot at home during those first years of high school. I would try to fit into all sorts of different friend groups: Am I a nerd? Am I sort of bad, yet cool? Am I artsy? It didn't matter that the people in these groups were nice—I am not a one-size-fits-all type of girl. I remember my parents offering that I could switch schools so I could start fresh. Instead—incredibly, for a girl at that age, in that environment—I decided I needed to be who I was no matter the circumstances and learn how to survive and be happy. By the middle of my junior year and beyond, I had created my own small group of random girls that came together and became best friends. This one choice became the foundation for my life. No matter my fears, no matter my circumstances, I would push through and remain true to who I was until I could right my own ship and sail in calmer waters. This has been the anchoring foundation for my life. Choosing to live this way takes incredible courage. It is not easy. And there have been times I made choices that were just "easier" or out of fear. Those never ended well.

Later, I had to make tough choices to save my own life. Choices that had major collateral damage, such as my divorce. My marriage did not have any obvious drama. I did not have a husband with a substance abuse problem; he did not abuse me. Simply, he was not right for me, and I was not right for him. I couldn't grow, I wasn't understood for who I was, and I was becoming more and more depressed. My children were seven and nine and I loved them more than anything in this world. You would describe me as an over-nurturer. The last thing I could ever imagine was ripping their world apart in order to save myself. But if I didn't save myself, if I didn't (as we learn in every flight we take) put on my mask first, I could not save them. I could not be a deeply understanding, loving mother for my children if I wasn't that for myself. I could not teach my children to be who they are no matter what, to live their lives, and not hold back if I couldn't do that myself. It was a heart-wrenching decision, one that I did not do quickly or take lightly but knew it had to be done.

And I remember Scarlett telling me that one of the things I was teaching my children was if you are not happy, it is possible to change your circumstances and your life, no matter how hard it might be. And it is up to you to do it. I knew it would be devastating to my children. And I also knew that as they grew up, I could teach them they would ultimately be responsible for how they decided to move through their own lives, handling the trauma of divorce and moving on from that. But the anchoring basis of my life, learned back in my childhood, is any fear can be conquered. You have to face the beast. You may have to fight. You may have to get bloody. You may fall down and feel like fear is winning. But there is always another breath, another surge of adrenaline to keep you alive.

Right around the time of my divorce, my life changed and at that time, I had no idea what this change meant. Or how momentous this change would be. I was visiting friends in San Francisco. I wanted to start meditating again however I always felt I was "doing it wrong." My mind never seemed to shut up and every time I tried to meditate; I would inevitably sit there running through my problems in my head until the timer went off.

I decided to find a meditation teacher so this time around, I could "do it right." I did what most modern humans do: I Google searched "meditation teachers near me"—meaning near where I lived, back East—and came upon a woman who not only taught meditation, but also Nia. The word "Nia" caught my eye, though I had no idea what that was, because about a week before I learned that Nia in Swahili meant aim or purpose. I was very drawn to that word and found it serendipitous that it would come up during my Google search for a meditation teacher. "This is a sign," I thought. So, I scheduled a session with Scarlett for when I returned home.

The rest, as it is said, is history. From that very first session, she taught me about the difference between myself and my mind. That I am not my mind. That my mind creates certain stories based on all my experiences and I live from those stories. If I want to change how I am feeling, then I need to create new stories from which to live. Where do I get these new stories, I wondered? Working with Scarlett, I learned the stories I was telling myself were not my own at all. They were the stories and messages I heard from others. It was those stories that had created who I had become.

The problem was, I was not happy, and my true self was not reflected in those old stories. One by one, we examined my beliefs about myself and where those beliefs came from.

Then we examined if each belief was true or not. 100% of the time, the belief was not my own and was not true. We began to uncover my own truth. And Scarlett taught me how to start living from my own, true story because that is the real story of who I am.

What about learning meditation? Isn't that the reason I went there? Scarlett taught me many variations of meditation, practices which do not only involve silencing the mind. Through my meditation practice, I could feel the difference between myself and my mind. And with that insight, I was able to realize I was already perfect, and the work is to adjust the mind.

After a few years of being Scarlett's client, we decided to go out for tea socially, another day that changed my life forever. Small moments of your life can change you forever and, in those moments, you may have no idea! We became close friends and started working together to help others achieve what I had achieved.

Oh, and yes, I did find out what Nia was and took a class to check it out!

CHAPTER 1

The "M" Word— Meditation for All!

"Rather than being your thoughts and emotions, be the awareness behind them."

—ECKHART TOLLE

PART 1
Phoenix

WE CAN'T ALWAYS CHANGE the circumstance we're currently in, but we can learn how to take charge of ourselves and show up in those circumstances powerfully. Meditation is one of the best, most powerful tools to help us do just that. Meditation is a way we can give our adult selves a TIME-OUT!

Ahhh...meditation. Seems we are hearing about it constantly these days. And here I am, bringing it up again. Good news! Meditation does not have to mean sitting down in silence and trying to quiet the mind. For those of you who have tried that and wound up saying "Well, meditation is clearly not for me," or "Meditation is just not my thing," welcome to a new world!

Meditation literally changes the brain and blood flow and unhooks us from panic, and flight or fight mode. With continued practice, your brain actually gets bigger. Like working a muscle with weights, we work our brain with breathing and meditation.

For me—on my journey to *learn to meditate*—I discovered that meditation could take many forms. And whatever form it takes for you, you can have success.

Here is what I realized about the importance of meditation and **what you can achieve** by practicing it every day for at least one minute per day!

- **A connection to the inner world inside yourself.** Have you ever been somewhere that is very loud and have said, "I can't even hear myself think!"? Meditation allows you to create a space where you can quiet down enough to not only hear yourself think, but you will also be able to observe your thoughts. This act of simply observing what you are thinking instead of getting hooked into those thoughts IS meditation. Think of it this way; meditation is like standing on the shoulder of a highway, watching the cars go by. Actively engaging in thoughts is like getting into each of the cars. Meditation is watching the cars go by without getting in—observing each thought as it goes by.

- **A mini *time-out*.** Everyone talks about giving children a time-out when they are overstimulated and acting out. There are days I would love someone to order me into time-out! A time to close the door and settle down in quiet peace. Sounds amazing to me. Well, that's exactly what you are giving yourself when you meditate. And you can control the amount of time you spend in *time-out*.

- **Clarity!** Whether we are deep in meditation for 30 minutes, or a quick time-out for five minutes, we now have a chunk of time to disconnect and, upon reconnection, gain clarity about what is happening around us and what we truly want. We jump off the bike, so to speak; look at the bike, see where it's headed, and decide if we are going in the direction we want to go. And when we jump back on the bike, we suddenly notice the beautiful surroundings that, just minutes before, we had passed by, unnoticed. We allow ourselves to live in the moment, because we realize that each moment we are in—our Present—is the only moment we can control. We don't control the Past or Future! And with that understanding comes peace. Trust me, the Past is done, history written. This cannot be changed no matter how many times we go over and over it in our minds. And we don't have any control over what will happen in the future. Only in the PRESENT MOMENT can we take actions that may influence our future or experience any reconciliation with our Past.

- **Rest!** A five-minute meditation, many experts say, is like taking a 20-minute nap. Many times, throughout my busy day—you too?—I could use a 20-minute power nap. I doubt I could get away with napping on the job. Instead, I close my door, put on my headphones, and meditate for five minutes. I come out of it refreshed and peaceful and ready to go. It is quite amazing. And nobody notices a five-minute break. You could be in the bathroom or on a call—whatever works!

In my therapy practice, I have a client, whom I will call Jennifer. (Names have been changed.) Jennifer had a lot of trauma growing up and came to me with what she referred to as "crippling anxiety and failed relationships" which left her feeling unloved and unworthy.

In our sessions, I offered her several different guided journeys and meditations for her to do in between sessions. Jennifer did none of them. She explained that when she attempted to meditate, her mind would race and she would get scared and overwhelmed, so she would stop for fear all the memories would come up and she would drown in her emotions.

In one of our sessions, I had Jennifer close her eyes. I asked her where she felt her anxiety the most. She said she felt it in her chest like someone was squeezing it hard. I asked her to close her eyes and drop down into her chest. She could not. She said it was way too dark and scary in there. I then asked her to imagine I had a headlamp on, and the light was shining like an x-ray into her chest. I asked her to imagine she was me, with the headlamp on, and tell me what she saw. After a while on this journey, Jennifer said she saw her heart as a dark tunnel. After some time journeying together in this frightening tunnel, she saw her scared, younger self curled up in a ball afraid to come out. Then, she noticed a door into a little room, and she invited her trembling, younger self to go in.

Inside were three of her adult friends who love her very much and appreciate all she has to offer in the world. She imagined her friends hugging and loving her younger afraid self, telling her all the things she never heard as a child. But Jennifer was not yet ready to come out of the little room. So, her meditation practice every day was to close her eyes, play music she loves, place her hands on her heart and feel the love her friends are giving young Jennifer in that room. I suggested she start with one minute and see how it went day by day.

Yes, this is meditation! Eventually, young Jennifer came to understand she is a loving, smart, beautiful little girl—a strong girl—who can come bravely out into the uncertain world. And after some time and daily practice, the adult Jennifer began to feel the same.

The more you practice, the more benefits you will find. Your intuition will get heightened, which will help in all areas of your life. You will notice you are more in control of your emotions and have developed your ability to respond calmly to situations where before you would have gotten triggered. When we remain calm in stressful situations, it helps us make better decisions. Just remember, you can design a practice that works for you: there's no one-size-fits-all meditation!

My daily meditation practice is ever-changing, based on new things I learn, or how I am feeling that day. I usually start my meditation with "heart breathing"—a five-minute guided breathing exercise designed to deeply relax. After that, I sit and listen to beautiful music. Because I have done the breathing practice, my mind has quieted down, and I can journey to the places I love. In those places, I discover clarity and understanding about different aspects of my life. Sometimes I meditate in the morning when I have time. Sometimes I meditate in between my two jobs to clear my head and give myself that needed little boost to transition to the next thing on my schedule.

Some meditation practices involve walking and paying careful attention to everything around you. I have a client who found her favorite way of meditating is chanting or repeating a word like "OM" and then practicing a moving meditation like *Tai Chi* or *Qi Gong*.

Walking meditations can be amazing! You can listen to meditative music as you walk, try a guided walking meditation, or just use mindfulness to listen, see, feel, and smell with every single step. *Be* in the present moment.

Hopefully, this will inspire you to take on some sort of meditative practice. Once you do, you will connect more and more to the Golden Buddha that is inside you. By developing your own relationship with meditation, you will come to know who you truly are and be able to see the mud for what it is.

And you will find you have the skills to start removing it, piece by piece.

PART 2
Scarlett

GOING DEEPER AND PUTTING
THE "M" WORD, MEDITATION,
INTO PRACTICE

MEDITATION AND DEEP BREATHING give you the power to take charge of your life and choose how you show up in it, moment to moment. It puts you back in the driver's seat. When you notice you're in flight or fight mode, you have the tools to pause, remember you have power over this reaction, take a deep breath and remind yourself you're in charge.

With practice, you form a new neural pathway to send a calming message to the limbic brain that you're safe. It can stand down. It is so empowering to be able to take charge of your mind and reactions in this way. You are training your mind to behave the way you want it to. This is how we shift the dynamic of a mind-dominated life where the mind and thoughts are in control of our emotions and reactions, to a heart-centered life where the authentic self is taking charge and teaching the mind what it is allowed to do.

Have you ever thought of that before? That you have a choice of what you allow your mind to think?

This idea opens us to the awareness that we are more than our thoughts and mind. We are deeper. We are heart and soul.

When you take charge of your mind, you can choose how you want to utilize this powerful tool. Often, we mistake the tool for the worker. We believe the mind is in charge, the mind is controlling the show. In reality, we're giving power to the mind unconsciously. Most of us haven't been taught we have a choice and control over what our mind does and thinks. When we live a mind-dominated life, we give away our power to the external circumstances the mind obsesses over and is influenced by. We become a slave to our own minds. True power is achieved when we shift the dominance from mind to heart. When heart is in charge, it can teach the mind what it's allowed to do and create for us. When I say heart, I'm referring to the higher self, the deeper self, the one that realizes the mind is not all that we are.

At some point in our lives, many of us realize we are on the wrong path. You may wake up at night and wonder how you got here, and where you're going. This is often the impetus to seek out meditation. You feel disconnected and far from your heart's goals and dreams because of the chaos of mind taking you in a direction you don't want to go. This often results in anxiety, depression, and feelings of helplessness, which then may be medicated with drugs or require years of therapy.

CHAOTIC MIND, CHAOTIC LIFE. CALM MIND, CALM LIFE

Each time you practice meditation, you're stepping outside of the momentum your mind has created. You are sending a strong message to mind that you are taking back your power to choose the direction your life is heading. You can re-energize your dreams and desires for the life you imagined. Each meditation lays down new pathways for the mind to use. You are literally re-patterning the landscape of your neural map.

There are decades of scientific research on the powerful effects of meditation. What do you want to feel in your life? What quality of life do you want to cultivate and grow? Asking yourself these questions will help you to design your practice and enjoy the effects that science is now validating with research. Mystics have known for centuries how to strengthen their minds and connect to their heart's desires. In these next exercises, you will create your practice and cultivate the skill to live this powerful life.

CREATING A MEDITATION SPACE

Your first exercise is setting up a sacred space, a meditation space for yourself, where you can relax, breathe, and unplug for a while. This is a place where you can easily practice without interruption or distraction. It can be just the corner of a room, say, your bedroom, or if you have the space, an entire room. It doesn't have to be big or elaborate, the objective is to have a quiet space with items that are meaningful and "sacred" to you; things that give you comfort. You might include candles, incense, a cloth on which to place sacred objects, perhaps some crystals or stones you've collected, statues, tarot cards, or images of symbols that evoke calm or spiritual connection.

Allow yourself some time to create this space. It feels good to honor yourself in this way. And it's fun! There is no right or wrong way to do this, just allow your heart and creativity to guide you.

An important piece to consider is what you will sit on and lie down on during meditation. Will you have a meditation cushion, pillows, chair, or blankets? Consider how important your physical comfort is and honor yourself during this process. If you feel more comfortable meditating in a chair, that's perfectly fine. If you're comfortable on a floor cushion or pillow, that's fine too.

Meditation music is also a wonderful way to create a peaceful energy in the space and bring relaxation and ease to your body and mind. There are many resources on YouTube, Pandora, and Spotify, for example, for you to explore and choose from. Your space may shift and change as you go through this journey to reflect your growth and what you are uncovering. It's like a living mandala of you.

Once you have your space set up, you're ready for your first meditation. Wear comfortable clothes so you can sit without restriction. Take off your shoes and put your phone away or on silent. If you're using your phone to play music, put it on "Do Not Disturb" so you can fully allow this time to be just for yourself.

We'll start with a simple ten-minute meditation to introduce you to mindfulness and self-awareness. When you want to feel calm and grounded this is the perfect tool. If your mind wanders, don't worry or get frustrated. This is very natural and will become less frequent as you develop your practice. Just notice your thoughts are wandering and bring your attention gently back to yourself. We want to be very gentle with ourselves, so our practice also teaches us to cultivate patience and kindness towards ourselves.

MEDITATION
THIS IS ME

Sit quietly and notice how your body is feeling. Are you comfortable? Adjust your position so your weight is evenly distributed, and your spine is straight. Imagine your head is a helium balloon tied to a string anchored to the ground. Your hands are in your lap and relaxed, either resting together in a bowl position or separated with each hand resting on your thighs. If you're sitting in a chair, have your feet firmly planted on the ground and feel the earth under each foot from toes to heels. Connect with the earth under you. If you're sitting on a cushion or on the ground, you can be cross-legged with your tailbone and hips connecting to the earth.

With your eyes closed or your gaze lowered, take a moment to notice your amazing body from head to toe, softening your thoughts, thanking your body for all the ways it keeps you healthy. Give yourself this message, either aloud or silently: "Thank you, body, I appreciate you."

Now, imagine or sense your body is a strong, sturdy tree growing beside a pristine lake or stream. Your legs and feet are the roots of this tree. Imagine them growing down from your feet into the earth, keeping you grounded and sturdy, while your arms and head are the branches reaching to the sun and sky. Feel open, expansive, breathing in life.

Take a moment to connect with this image and sensation, feeling both grounded and expansive.

We're going to connect to our breath now. Bring your attention to the gentle rise and fall of your lungs. Simply noticing, follow each breath, like waves of the ocean, the breath comes in without effort, and the breath releases, without effort.

There is nothing to hold on to. You receive what you need and release naturally what you don't need. Follow the natural cycle of your breath. With no effort, your body breathes. Become aware, this is me: breathing. Receive as you inhale. Release as you exhale. Sense your lungs and belly filling, expanding as you receive and contracting as you release.

After 20 or 30 breaths, with eyes still closed or gaze lowered, take a moment to notice your bodily sensations. What are you feeling? Simply notice: give your body a moment of attention and recognition, no judgment, just simply noticing.

And with five more mindful breaths, receiving and releasing, we're going to connect back to the image and sensation of the tree, grounded, steady, and strong. Feel or imagine the tree roots coming back up and settling into your feet. You are connected to the earth. Sense or imagine the tall branches, coming down to settle into your head and shoulders. Feel yourself connected to the sky and expansive Universe; experience the trunk of the tree as your spine, holding you tall, strong, and steady as you move through your day. Think, or say, This is me: connected, strong, steady; receiving and releasing.

When you feel ready, gently open your eyes. Take a moment to connect to the space. Take a deep, energizing breath. Give your legs, torso, and arms gentle taps or smooth strokes to bring yourself fully back—and smile.

This is me.

Next, let's journal about this experience!

Ask yourself these, or other questions that you feel drawn to ask yourself... and answer, in your journal.

What sensations did I feel?
What images did I see?
What did it feel like to notice my breath?
How was it to sit with receiving and releasing with no effort?

Write any other insights, feelings, or sensations you experienced.

A calm mind makes it easier to access creative solutions. Stress, fear, and anger impede blood flow to our brain, decreasing our ability to think clearly and make good decisions. This is why meditation and deep breathing are so important.

Meditation and mindful breathing give us a practice of pausing and this unleashes the power to take charge of our life and how we show up in it, moment to moment.

PROCESS
4/7/8 BREATHING

This exercise is a short breathing meditation and works wonders when you need to take a break before responding to someone, or before making a presentation, or anytime you just need to get grounded and centered quickly. It is a short mindful breathing exercise to calm the nervous system, lower blood pressure, and give you a moment to ground yourself when you feel overwhelmed or stressed.

- Inhale through your nose for the count of 4, filling your lungs and belly. Pull your shoulders back, tilt your chin up, and feel your heart and lungs open.
- Hold your breath for the count of 7. Feel the expansion and fullness of receiving this life-giving oxygen.
- Exhale through your mouth slowly and deliberately for the count of 8. Feel the ability to release consciously and completely, emptying everything out.
- Squeeze all the air out of your belly until it's completely empty.
- Then begin again. Become very aware of each feeling, receiving what you need as you inhale for the count of 4; enjoying what you have and appreciating the fullness as you hold for the count of 7; then release consciously what you don't need any longer for the count of 8.
- Count in your mind: 4, 7, 8. This keeps the mind occupied and keeps you on track.
- Repeat five times or more, as needed.

If you feel lightheaded, just pause, and return to your natural breath, then start over.

This may happen from an abundance of oxygen as you inhale more deeply than usual. It should pass quickly as you pause for a moment.

This is a great little mindful moment you can do all through the day as needed or any time you need to bring awareness to the present moment.

MEDITATION
JOURNEY TO YOUR SANCTUARY

This can be used alone for a peaceful and relaxing meditation or as a starter for other healing journeys.

Start by sitting or lying down comfortably and noticing your breath; the coolness on your nostrils as you inhale; the warmth on your upper lip as you exhale. If your mind wanders during this or any of the meditations, just gently bring your thoughts back as often as you need. With practice, your mind will know what you want it to do and will stop wandering as much.

Relax your whole body, starting with your feet and legs. Exhale and allow your feet and legs to get heavy and to rest. Notice your hips and belly softening and relaxing with each breath. Now pay attention to your back muscles and your spine relaxing. If there is any tension or tightness in your shoulders and neck, allow it to melt down your arms and out your fingertips. Finally, notice your head relaxing and melting any tension from your forehead and brow. Release your jaw and allow your teeth to separate as your whole face relaxes. Move down your throat, into your chest. Notice the rise and fall of your inhale and exhale. With no effort, your body is breathing. Notice or imagine the beating of your own heart.

Now, imagine your heart center opening and illuminating a pathway—your heart's path of love and peace. Sense yourself moving down this pathway, noticing what you see and feel around you on your path of love. At the end of the pathway is a gate, when you are ready, push open the gate and take three steps down... 1... 2... 3...

Step into the landscape that opens before you. Explore what you see and feel around you in this safe, peaceful space. It may be a place you've been before or a brand-new place you are seeing for the first time. Take time to explore and feel the love and safety around you.

What do you see? Feel? Hear? What colors or textures? Fully experience this wonderful, peaceful space and enjoy being here. As you relax more fully, sense yourself releasing all the tension and stress you've been carrying and feel it melting away as if you're emptying out your body and mind. Each exhale releases stress; each inhale brings in lightness and peace until your whole body and mind are glowing from the light within. Notice how it feels to give yourself permission to let this all go.

Relax here as long as you like; there is no rush.

As you complete the meditation, make your way back across your landscape with renewed energy and focus. Notice how you feel as you come up the three steps, pass through your gate and step back onto your heart's path that brought you here. Finally, come back into your body, rest in your heart center and notice what you're feeling now.

Take a deep breath. Wiggle your fingers and toes. Gently open your eyes.

Take a few moments to journal about your journey.

Ask and answer these and any questions that come up for you:

What did your landscape look and feel like?

What stood out for you?

What did you feel or sense emotionally, mentally, and physically as you journeyed

CHAPTER 2

I Am Not My Feelings

*"I am not my thoughts, feelings, circumstances
of changing events in life,
I am the awareness, the alertness, the changeless
which remains present behind it."*
—MARCUS THOMAS

PART 1
Phoenix

I AM NOT MY feelings. When did I first understand what that means? Because I feel things, in my heart, my body, and my head so strongly—I could not understand what that meant. Until someone told me this:

As humans, unlike most creatures living on earth, we can observe our thoughts and see how each thought makes our body feel. I can think, "I am absolutely useless. I don't even see the point of being alive." Observing that thought, I feel sad, and hopeless, as though I am falling into a deep dark abyss.

I can think, "I am truly wonderful. I am a strong, loving person who finds the fun and light in life and shares it with as many people as possible: I try to ease the suffering of others." Observing that thought, I feel a surge of happiness, purpose, and peace.

Understanding all of this—observing and feeling the feelings I am choosing to evoke—helps me realize the true "me" cannot be these thoughts or the feelings that follow. If I *was* my thoughts and my feelings, I would not be able to observe them. Clearly, I am only *their observer*.

Here is another example. Imagine the blue sky. The blue sky is always there, every single day. When we look up at a beautiful clear blue sky, we may feel peaceful or happy or whatever feelings a clear blue sky conjures up for you.

Now imagine some white puffy clouds. We can still see the blue sky beneath and around the clouds. We know it is still there. How do you feel when you look up and see some clouds? Do you go into your imagination and see elephants and dragons? Do you feel whimsical, childlike? Are you anxious because it might get cloudier?

Now imagine a day filled with white clouds, no blue shining through. How do you feel when you look up at the sky? Does it make you feel sad because it's a dreary day? Happy because you love rain and maybe it will rain? And let me ask you: is the blue sky still there beneath the white clouds? Of course, it is. Since we don't see it there, we *forget* to see it.

The blue sky is our true selves. It is constant and never changing. It remains still and clear and beautifully blue. And the clouds are our thoughts. With each cloud comes a new thought, and with each thought may come a new feeling or emotion. We have so many thoughts and feelings all day long that we forget that our true selves, our unchanging self, our perfect golden self, is there, beneath the thoughts, beneath the feelings.

Give yourself some time to let this sink in. Begin to observe your thoughts and the feelings that follow. And while this is happening, connect with the unchanged safety of your blue sky. Practice this.

My client RJ gets triggered when she is with her mother. All her mother has to do is say something like, "Are you going to wear THOSE shoes with that dress?" and RJ goes into an angry fit. Drowning in her anger, she feels small and stupid and not good enough. She doubts herself. Is she an angry person who is small and stupid and worthless? Where is this coming from?

She is a clear blue sky before going to see her mother. Her mother comments on her shoes, and she is immediately angered. When we look deeper together, she realizes when her mother criticizes her in any way, it immediately brings her back to her childhood when her mother dressed her in dresses, and she did not like that. She wanted to wear comfortable pants and clothes. She felt her mother dressed her up in the version she wanted her to be and never saw her for who she was.

When she gets triggered and angry, her thoughts connect back to her childhood, and she feels the same feelings she did then. In a split second, the sky becomes cloudy, and she forgets who she is and only sees herself for the clouds. Sees herself as the anger, the shame, the unworthiness. But is she those things? Of course not. She just forgot she is the blue sky. Trigger, thoughts, feelings, forget. Trigger, thoughts, feelings, forget. Trigger, thoughts, feelings, forget. All-day long, every day.

I'm pretty sure we all find it exhausting! It's literally like a roller coaster of ups and downs of emotions and physical sensations. The truth is, we can get off the roller coaster, float in the blue sky and watch the ride without getting on. Is it easy? No, of course not, or we would all be blissful all the time! But can we start incorporating it into our lives slowly? *Yes.* And each time we remember our blue sky, our thoughts and emotions become our choice. We can't get rid of the negative thoughts, or they will try even harder to stay. Instead, we can gently notice them. We can see them as the clouds and understand we are not them, but they are part of our human experience. And we are supposed to learn from them. They are our teachers.

RJ learned much in that session, as we examined her reaction. It was a huge *Ah ha!* experience which shifted her. And that becomes one of many experiences which grow us. And that is the point. The more of these moments we have, the more time we spend as the blue sky. Some days we connect to our blue sky more than others. And that is okay. As long as we know it is there, behind whatever it is we are thinking and feeling, we can always come back to it. And we won't get consumed by the clouds.

During my divorce, there were some days I felt overwhelmed and sad, and guilty. My thoughts were, "How can I do this to my children?" "How can I do this to my husband? I must be so selfish." On those days, I remember sitting on my bathroom floor with the fan running, crying, and crying, curled up in pain. I allowed my pain to flow. I knew I was there underneath, unchanged, and perfect. It was just so hard to go there. But when I let the thoughts come in, when I let the pain rack my body and flow out through my tears, the pain passed. I didn't try to stop it. I knew I was not my pain. After these emotions passed, I would feel tired and relieved. And then I could see other clouds, hear other thoughts of "I will never fully grow into who I am supposed to be if I stay. I will never be happy. That is not fair to me, my children, or my husband. I must save myself if I want to be a great mother and reach my full potential in this life." I would gain strength from that: I would feel a deeper connection to my blue sky—my true self.

PART 2

Scarlett

GOING DEEPER AND PUTTING
I AM NOT MY FEELINGS
INTO PRACTICE

THIS CHAPTER HELPS US to release the fear that comes with having difficult emotions. When we're feeling sad or depressed, we can feel like this will never go away. The pain may be very intense and can feel scary, but when we know it's not forever, we can relax into the experience and trust it will pass. Using the tools and processes you learn in this chapter can help make the difficult feelings pass more easily. We will also make the distinction between what we feel and who we are

What do we do with difficult emotions? Sometimes, it can seem like we're drowning in sadness, depression, anxiety, or anger. In that moment, the emotions can feel overwhelming.

Is there any emotion that stays the same forever? When you're sad or angry, do you feel that way forever? Or does another emotion take its place eventually?

Within one day, you may have 20 emotions. For example, when you wake up you may feel irritated; when you get to work or school, you may feel happy to see your co-workers or friends; at lunchtime, you may get into an argument with someone and feel angry; later in the day, you spend time with your partner and may feel relaxed and happy.

Every emotion we experience has an ebb and flow, up and down. We would love to feel happy and relaxed all the time, but even these feelings don't last permanently. Whether we're sad, angry, insecure, happy, excited, tired, or discouraged, all of these are feelings and will flow through us. No single emotion is permanent. This is important to remember when we feel unpleasant or difficult emotions. I've found it helpful to say to myself, *this will pass, it's just an emotion and all emotions come and go.*

> *Our feelings are a reflection of our thoughts. If we don't like the way we are feeling, we can shift our thoughts to create the desired feeling state.*

When you're experiencing challenging feelings, you can recognize that you are more than your feelings.

Such as, when we say, "I'm depressed," it states we *are* depression. But is that true? You are feeling depressed, but when that feeling passes you will be the one still there.

There is a deeper part of all of us that stays the same no matter what we're feeling. That's the part of us that can tell our minds we are more than our feelings.

Shifting the language we use and the relationship we have to what we are feeling is very powerful. For example, try shifting from the thought, "I'm anxious" to "At this moment, I *feel* anxious." Words are very powerful, and how we choose them has a direct impact on our state of mind and body.

It's a powerful practice to remind yourself that you are more than your emotions. Emotions come and go. You are the one noticing your emotions and thoughts. We can name this part of you "The Witness" or "The Watcher."

Take a moment now for a mindfulness meditation designed to help you notice different aspects of yourself.

- Take three deep breaths in through your nose and release them slowly through your mouth.
- Notice how your body feels.
- What emotions are you feeling right now?
- Rest your attention on the thoughts going through your mind. Just notice, don't try to change anything.
- Then ask yourself: who is the one noticing all of what's going on? Who is the noticer? Who is the one witnessing what I am thinking and feeling?

Just from this simple practice alone, we cultivate the awareness that we are more than our mind and body. There is a deeper, bigger aspect of us behind the scenes of our day-to-day life. It is connecting to this part of us that will enable us to regulate and bring harmony to the many parts of ourselves.

With practice, we can cultivate curiosity by asking, "Why am I feeling this way?" Take a step back and notice the emotion and ask, "Where did you come from?" Sometimes we don't know why we feel what we're feeling. We may not be able to pinpoint where it's coming from yet. But the good news is—we don't have to know its origin to be able to take charge of it.

MEDITATION
I AM

This next meditation brings us more in tune with who we are underneath the emotions we are feeling.

Have your journal and pen and an extra sheet of paper ready—you are going to create a new statement or contract about who you are.

Begin by sitting or lying down comfortably, focusing on your breath, noticing the coolness on your nostrils as you inhale, and the warmth on your upper lip as you exhale.

Relax your whole body, starting with your feet and legs. With your next exhale, allow your feet and legs to get heavy and to rest.

Notice your hips and belly softening and relaxing with each breath. Now, pay attention to your back muscles and the length of your spine relaxing, if there is any tension or tightness in your shoulders and neck, allow it to melt down your arms and out your fingertips.

Finally, notice your head relaxing. Melting any tension from your forehead and brow, release your jaw and allow your teeth to separate as your whole face relaxes. Moving down your throat and into your chest, notice the rise and fall of your inhale and exhale. With no effort, your body is breathing. Notice or imagine the beating of your own heart.

Now, imagine your heart center opening and illuminating a pathway. This is your path of heart, of love, and peace.

Sense yourself moving down this pathway, noticing what you see and feel around you on your path of love.

At the end of the pathway is a gate, when you are ready, push open the gate and take three steps down, 1, 2, 3, and onto the landscape of your sacred space. Explore what you see and feel around you in this safe, peaceful space. It may be a place you've been before or a brand-new place you are creating now. Take time to explore and feel the love and safety that is around you.

What do you see? Feel? Hear? What colors or textures?

Fully experience this wonderful, peaceful space and enjoy being here. As you more fully relax, sense any tension or stress you've been carrying just releasing and melting away as if you're emptying out your body and mind. Each exhale releases stress; each inhale brings in lightness and peace until your whole body and mind are glowing from the light within.

Now, notice that someone is walking toward you; they look intriguing and feel safe and comfortable.

As they approach, you notice it is *you*. This is the highest, clearest version of yourself. Take some time to notice what you see, feel, and perceive from this version of yourself.

How does this version of you dress? How do you walk and carry yourself? What is the feeling or vibe you give off?

Take some time to notice what your qualities and strengths are.

What traits do you notice? What do you see in your eyes?

Spend a few moments with this version of you; get to know this other version of yourself. *Feel* what it's like to be with this person.

You can ask yourself questions, for example:

How can I stay anchored to the strengths I see in you?
What causes me to get off track or consumed by my emotions?
Is there any wisdom or advice you have for me today?
What do I need to release or receive to move forward in my life?

As you complete this journey, notice the landscape surrounding you on the way back. Is anything different, has anything changed in the way it looks or feels?

Coming back down the path of heart that brought you here, settle back into your heart center; gently coming back to the body, connecting to the breath

Take a deep breath. Wiggle your fingers and toes and gently open your eyes

Then, on the paper you set out, write in big letters on top, *I AM*, and list all the qualities you saw in yourself. Remember what it felt like to be with that version of you; what was the feeling, the look, the strengths that you saw and felt. When you are finished writing all the *I AM* statements, write details in your journal of what you experienced.

You have just uncovered and connected with a deep truth. Keep a copy of this statement, this new contract, next to your bed and read it before sleep and first thing in the morning. This is how we train our minds to focus on how we choose to live and what our higher truth is. This is a very powerful process.

PROCESS
NOTICE THE ONE THINKING

We are not our thoughts. We are the one thinking the thoughts. We can choose to think whatever we want.

To begin, get comfortable and relaxed. Notice what your mind is thinking without trying to change it. Whatever your mind is thinking, just acknowledge it. "Oh, my mind is thinking _____." Then watch the next thought come and acknowledge that one. Stay with this for a minute or two.

Then, ask the question, "Am I my thoughts?" If not, why not?

Ask "Who is the one noticing the thoughts? The thinker behind the thoughts—who is that?"

Once you acknowledge who the thinker is, close your eyes again. This time, when you notice what your mind is thinking, ask "Do I have to think this thought?" Connect with your ability to choose what you think. Try thinking differently, creating a positive thought. Such as, "I accept myself just as I am right now," or "I am in charge of my life." Notice how it feels to consciously create a thought. How is that different from the endless flow of unconscious thoughts?

This exercise emphasizes we have a choice. We are not victims or slaves to our thoughts. We are the thinker, not the thought. We have the power to teach our minds to think whatever we choose. Initially, you may not be able to hold onto the chosen thought for long, but with practice, you will build a new "mental muscle" to create from.

Louise Hay, prolific writer—and queen of affirmations—taught us that at the start, we may have to repeat an affirmation 1000 times a day to train our minds to think a new thought. After a while, we may need to repeat it 500 times a day. After another while, it may be only 100 times a day and eventually, the new thought will be natural, and we won't have to remind ourselves any longer. This is where dedication and commitment to the new way of living are so important. We must stay connected to how we would prefer to feel in our lives and use the tools to achieve it.

Another aspect of training our minds to think differently is to heal the original wounding causing the painful or limiting thoughts we carry.

Often, at the moment we experience hurt or trauma, the wounded part of us "freezes" in time. Other aspects of us grow and mature naturally, but these wounded parts may stay stuck at the very age when they were traumatized and then show up later in our lives with all the unhealed hurt and fear they still experience as if the wound is current.

For example, I went to a Catholic elementary school. When I was in second grade, my teacher told me to stand up and read a paragraph aloud to the class. I was nervous and embarrassed at being everyone's focus. After I read a couple of lines, I stumbled on a word and then got even more nervous, which made me stumble even more. I remember my face getting red and my body getting all hot and numb. Everyone was staring at me, and it made me so uncomfortable. At that point, the nun, with exasperation and impatience, told me to sit down. I was so ashamed and traumatized. I criticized myself and spoke cruelly to myself. "You're so stupid! Why can't you do anything right? Everyone hates you!"

I swore I would never speak in front of people again. Throughout the remainder of school, I did everything I could to become invisible so I wouldn't get chosen to speak in class. It even affected me socially. I had severe social anxiety. I always stayed quiet in groups of friends, doubting my answers or comments, feeling insecure and stupid.

MEDITATION
BRINGING BACK THE WOUNDED SELF

When we experience trauma, the wounded part of us "freezes" in time. Other aspects of ourselves may grow and mature naturally, but these wounded parts of our consciousness may stay stuck at the very age when they were traumatized, and then show up later in our lives with all the unhealed hurt and fear those parts of us still believe they are experiencing. In the example of my trauma from second grade in Catholic school, I felt embarrassed, vulnerable, ashamed, and afraid of the judgment of others. I would continue to feel all these emotions each time I was asked to read aloud in school and into my adult life. It would show up when I had to speak to groups or teach a class. My seven-year-old self would reemerge, and I would experience all the same embarrassment, fear, and vulnerability as if I was back in that classroom.

Even when we don't remember the exact circumstance causing our current trigger, we can still have profound healing from this process.

To begin, connect with an emotional trigger you feel: fear, anxiety, insecurity, apathy; if possible, connect with a circumstance you remember where you still feel the hurt. This may be something you are carrying from your childhood, so try to go back as far as you can to when you first began to feel this wounding.

Notice where in your body you feel this. Is it in your chest, in your heart? In your stomach or throat? Notice how it shows up in your body right now. Rate the intensity of the feeling on a scale of 1-10, 1 being very low, and 10 being very high.

Now, journey to your **Sanctuary**. Relax here for a moment, and feel the safety and peace surrounding you.

When you feel ready, invite your wounded self into your **Sanctuary**. Notice how old you are. Take some time to talk kindly to this self, letting this self know she is safe now. Ask this self why she was hurt, and how. Who hurt her, what happened? Listen with gentleness and compassion.

Now, ask this part of you if she would like to come back with you. What does she need to feel safe and protected by her older self for her to grow up and join you in the present? Listen to her response; pay attention to how you can take care of her. She may ask to be loved and cared for as you would a child. She may want to do childlike, playful things to feel good about being free again.

This is our time to reconnect with this lost part of ourselves. It's a reunion filled with love and compassion. If this part of yourself wants to come back to the present with you, you may carry her or hold hands as you come back across your **Sanctuary**. If she is not ready to come back yet, ask what she would need to feel safe to stay present with you in your current life. Let her know that you honor her decision and that you will continue to hold and love her. You can revisit her again when you feel the time is right.

When you settle back into your body, if your wounded part comes back with you, imagine this part of you integrating into the area in your body where you felt the wounding: your heart, or your stomach—wherever you experienced these feelings. Allow the integration to heal your old trauma. There is no need to stay hidden and frozen in time. You are whole and safe now.

Before you open your eyes and come back into the room, rate the feeling in your body again from 1–10. Notice if the intensity has decreased in the part of your body where you were holding this hurt.

Take a few minutes to write about the journey and the part of you that has integrated back and healed. How will this affect you now in your present life? How can you continue to honor the part of you that came back? What does that part need to grow and feel safe?

If this soul part wasn't ready to come back just yet, write about the insights you gained from making this connection. What did she have to say to you about her wounding? What will she need to come back with you next time?

PROCESS
CREATING AFFIRMATIONS

Affirmations are positive statements you repeat to yourself to challenge the negative thought habits that have accumulated over time.

Practicing positive affirmations can be simple and fun, and all you need to do is pick a phrase and repeat it to yourself.

In this activity, we're going to create affirmations based on the meditations you've learned so far. These will keep you connected to the experience and help you develop new healthy and happy thought patterns.

For example:

I am safe and loved.
My mind and body are calm and peaceful.
I am like a tree with strong, steady roots keeping me grounded.
In every moment, I receive and release.
I release easily what no longer serves me.
I am more than my feelings. I am in charge of what I think and feel.

Take a moment to create your own affirmations and read them throughout the day. You can write them on sticky notes and place them around your home or put them on your home screen on your phone and computer, to remind yourself of your true value.

You have begun to take charge of your own experience and are expanding your capacity to choose how you want to feel.

You are starting to live life by your own design!

CHAPTER 3

Respond vs. React

"It's not the situation, but whether we react, or respond, to the situation that's important."

—ZIG ZIGLAR

PART 1

Phoenix

Respond vs. React: This concept was, and probably still is, one of the harder ones for me. It is *extremely* powerful when used; however, if you are anything like me—emotional, passionate about what is right, easily triggered when I feel that someone is trying to use their power or manipulate me—then this will be one of the more challenging aspects of responding instead of reacting to master. And I am still mastering it, even as I write about it! Just being honest.

Most of the time we move through life not noticing our thoughts or our minds. We have conversations and talk; we watch the news and think and talk. We go to work and do what we normally do, answering questions and creating the work we are hired to do. We don't stop and pause to constantly examine our every move to ensure we are aligned with how we think and how we want to feel. If we were to do that, it would be like constantly pushing pause on the television. Our main character wakes up, pauses to notice her thoughts, and shifts them to match how she wants to feel. She gets out of bed. Her boyfriend comes in and says, "Good morning." Again, hit pause; figure out what to say to best match her mood and the core of who she is. Hit play.

This is not real life. We move through life pretty much the opposite of play/pause/play. We wake up and react to our thoughts with our mood. We then react immediately to whoever speaks to us. If the dog immediately wants our attention and we are still foggy from sleep, we react right away, and sometimes, later, we feel bad about how we snapped at the loving pup. And on and on we go, moving through our day this way. Someone at the coffee shop cuts you off in line and is talking loudly on their cell phone; we react with anger and possibly argue with them, and our day seems to be off to a crappy start. Conversely, in the coffee shop, someone ahead of us pays for our coffee and we react with a feeling of gratitude. We offer thanks and our day feels great.

I have very strong feelings about a variety of topics. When I get triggered by someone, I don't take the time to think about why I am being triggered. I just put on my boxing gloves and enter the ring. You won't manipulate me or try to put someone down when I'm there! I will come at you full force until you realize just how wrong you are and just how strong I am. Afterward, I feel tired and emotionally drained. And once someone picks up on the things that trigger me, they are in control. They have the power. I fought to hold on to the power and now I have given it away.

When I look at **Respond vs. React** in this manner, it gives me the drive and determination to master this idea. *I DO NOT WANT TO GIVE MY POWER TO ANYONE!*

So, what is the difference between **Respond** and **React** anyway? When something happens and we feel triggered, an automatic reaction comes flying out of our mouths and bodies. No thinking, no pausing—just leap into action.

On the other hand, when that same trigger happens, instead of leaping into re-action, if we stop for a moment, we will notice that we have a *choice* in how we want to *respond* to the situation. We are always in control of ourselves and the way we want to handle the situation that best matches up with who we are and how we want to feel. When we feel calm, it is much easier to choose how we want to respond to something. Something that might be a small trigger—or not even a trigger at all—might just be something slightly controversial. We can take a breath and look at what's happening and cultivate our best response while remaining calm.

But what happens when our buttons get pushed? We usually dive right in and forget we have a choice. Button gets pushed and it's 0–60 in five seconds or less. Then we have lost. Whoever is the button pusher has taken control and they are leading us right where they want us. We are left feeling angry, sad, and exhausted. Angry at them for what they are doing or saying, angry at ourselves for reacting that way, and tired of the endless loop this ride takes us on.

So, what do we do? The good news is that though I am an emotional, passionate person, I have been able to learn and practice this *most* of the time. As I said before, I am still working on it. However, once you taste the power behind this technique, you will want more. You will feel so strong with your new ability to pause that reacting will feel like weakness.

Let me give you an example of how incredibly powerful this idea can be. I had a person in my life for some time who I could not remove for various reasons. Let's call this person *Mark*. Mark knew exactly how to push my buttons. Whenever we had to meet to discuss things, he would do a little joking, a little small talk to put me at ease, and then hit me with the trigger. And every time, I would bite. He was a very manipulative person and always tried to control me. Since that is my hot button issue, I would immediately fight back full force. And I am a great fighter. I am a great debater. My father is a lawyer and is constantly baffled by my not choosing to follow in his footsteps.

After many years of this manipulation by Mark, I had had it. I am not one to give away my power, but I did it again and again with him—until I was finally done. One day in late November, we decided to meet for coffee to talk. On the drive over to the coffee shop, I was talking out loud to the Universe—which is something I do when I need advice! I was saying I have to have Mark in my life, and I am done giving away my power each time we meet. What do I do? And suddenly a voice in my head said, "You don't have to answer right away."

YOU DON'T HAVE TO ANSWER RIGHT AWAY! Freaking brilliant! Why hadn't I thought of that before? You don't have to answer right away. Who knew? I always believed when someone was saying something unjust to you, you should fight back immediately.

Well, I know the breath is the key to calming our nervous system. So, I knew that in order to not answer right away, I would have to inhale deeply and slowly exhale before I spoke. Then it occurred to me, that I was going to a coffee shop! I could order a hot tea, and when I felt triggered, pretend to blow on the hot tea and breathe until I calmed down. I could reflect on what Mark said and then speak.

That is when I created **P.B.R.S.** (phonetically it sounds like Puhburbs). *P.B.R.S stands for* **Pause, Breathe, Reflect, Speak.** Now I had a plan. And—I was looking forward to our meeting so I could practice.

I entered the coffee shop and bought my tea. I sat down at the table across from Mark, already feeling nervous. I blew gently on my tea, cooling the tea and relaxing my nervous system.

Then he started to speak, and immediately I could feel my blood pressure rising. Deep breath, blow on the tea, calm the body. I did not interrupt him as I usually did. He kept talking. I kept discreetly breathing on my tea. When he was done, he said, "Well? What do you have to say?" I know he was poised and ready for the attack he wanted. I felt a calmness come over me. I said, "I heard what you said, and I will take time to think about it and get back to you." I thought his head was going to pop off his shoulders. He said, "You have nothing at all to say?" I said, "As I said, I am just hearing this and I will take time to think it over and get back to you. Is there anything else?" He looked stunned. He stammered and made some noises, and in a small voice said, "No." I said, "Okay then, goodbye."

I got up from the table, feeling like I was ten feet tall, and strolled out of the coffee shop. He was left sitting there, not knowing what to do or what just happened to him. It was *amazing*! I usually leave meetings with him angry and disgusted, but this time I was on top of the world! I did it! I **Responded** *rather than* **Reacted!** It was the best feeling. And later when I emailed him my response, it was well thought out and factual. Plus—he was not there trying to manipulate me by pushing my buttons. It was beautiful. So now I practice **P.B.R.S.** regularly. If sometimes I forget and I react immediately, I notice it and try to pause at that point in the argument. I am constantly working on this, and I am succeeding more often than not. And life feels good when you are in control of yourself and not giving away your power to whoever wants to take it.

So how do you start? One of the most important things is to notice your triggers and what the underlying fears are. For example, with Mark, he triggered me by creating a scenario he knew wasn't right or fair. My fear was being taken advantage of or being manipulated.

What core beliefs or values of yours are threatened when you are triggered? Once you start understanding what's behind your triggers, you become able to understand them and take a pause before you react. This can become a little game and when you succeed, you grow and find peace, instead of being led into the fight and left feeling deflated and exhausted.

PART 2
Scarlett

GOING DEEPER AND PUTTING
RESPOND VS. REACT
INTO PRACTICE

As we can see, we all have our trigger points; those big buttons that send us off the deep end and make us behave in ways that leave us shaking our heads afterward, wondering what happened to our common sense. Where do these come from and why are they so hard to control?

Our trigger points are the parts of our lives that are unresolved and looking for attention. They are the unhealed aspects of our story.

Each time something inflames us, these wounded parts take center stage, seeking attention, comfort, and healing. If ignored, they can take over our lives. For example, if you've had early childhood abandonment wounds then a boyfriend or girlfriend not responding to your text right away may seriously trigger you. You may make up a whole story in your mind of why they're not responding based on your fears, "'They're with someone else;'" "I knew this wouldn't last;'" "They're getting ready to break up with me;'" "How dare they ignore me!" This subjective thinking makes your old fears the center of the story with you in the role of victim.

The transformation to objective thinking happens when you're able to recognize you're being triggered by an old trauma or wound. Step back and take a breath; look at the circumstance from a more logical view. Maybe they're in a meeting and can't get to the phone. The phone may be off or in another room. Until you speak directly to them, you don't know what's happening on their end. But your fear and the negativity bias take over, making up stories that match what your past wounding felt like. When we're triggered and reacting from emotion, the mind is sending an *over-amplified* message of danger. We feel threatened by something that seems immediate and intense. The mind believes it's protecting us, preparing us for the worst so we won't get hurt again.

Our reactive triggers can also be expressed as anger masquerading as righteousness, a need to prove our point so we feel safe. Have you ever been in a heated argument and somewhere during it you wonder why you're even arguing? You realize you don't care that much about it, but you're compelled to drive home your point; you can't back down or let it go. In the heat of the moment, you feel a sense of power and the need to protect yourself by being right. This reaction is, again, the old, wounded self who seeks attention so it can be noticed and healed. Perhaps you feel disempowered or unheard in your life. Winning an argument can bring a feeling of strength and being validated but it's only momentary.

Recognizing what's happening on a deeper, energetic level when we get triggered is very powerful. When we can pause and receive the message the trigger is offering—though sometimes painful and uncomfortable—we take charge of our own mental and emotional health and create the possibility of healing. This is the first step in the healing process: notice what is happening on a deep level and recognize we have a choice of how we show up when we are triggered. It's like seeing bullies for what they are—hurt, afraid, and on the attack to protect themselves from a perceived threat.

The amygdala is the emotion center of the brain, located in the limbic system, the oldest part of the brain, which triggers our flight or fight response to perceived threats. As we evolve and expand our awareness, we teach the limbic system how we want it to behave. You can train the amygdala to calm down with meditation and higher reasoning. Research shows the amygdala will become smaller and less reactive and you'll experience more calm and confidence as the old story of wounding diminishes its hold on you.

With this knowledge of how to calm the amygdala, we open a new dialog with ourselves. "Okay, I recognize I'm reacting out of fear and the old story of hurt. I'm going to take a few breaths to give myself a little space and choose calm, rational thoughts right now." Without judging yourself, simply give your mind a new thought to focus on as you calm your nervous system and return to balance. You can create any mantra or phrase that feels calming to you, such as, "I'm calm and safe, everything is okay." Experiment with different phrases and see how they make you feel as you take charge of your reaction. In this way you are re-patterning your habits and creating new neural pathways, so the mind has another option when triggered. With practice and time, you will create your desired outcome, a calm response, rather than being trapped in your default mode of fear-based reaction.

Working on a cognitive level by rewiring your mental default mode and creating a calming dialog to redirect your thoughts and using the breath to give yourself some space provides you with practical tools to diffuse your reaction to the immediate trigger. To have a permanent transformation, we also need to heal the original point of fear at a deeper level. This approach utilizes the power of combining both the head and heart.

In this section, you'll find a healing process called **Disconnecting from Your Painful Past,** and as you practice this healing process you will transform and heal whatever's triggering you. You will be guided to disconnect the cords keeping you attached to that old story so your heart can gently heal, and you can feel free and strong again.

This is a powerful skill, shifting from *Reacting* to *Responding*, and it puts *you* in charge of creating a life you can live in a new, free, way. A chaotic mind creates a chaotic life; a calm mind creates a calm life. You will learn to calm your mind and heal your heart in the following processes.

"Every time you are tempted to respond in the same old way, ask if you want to be a prisoner of the past or a pioneer of the future."
—DEEPAK CHOPRA

MEDITATION
DISCONNECTING THE CORDS TO YOUR PAINFUL PAST

Often, when we are hurt by someone, we continue to give them our power and energy by staying emotionally attached to them or the situation. Our brain can become addicted to the pain and the old story, holding this wounding like a trophy. This keeps us trapped and stuck in that painful experience. The first step in healing is being willing to release what we have been holding onto. We need to connect with our desire to be free even while we may be afraid of letting go.

Give yourself twenty minutes of quiet time to practice *Disconnecting from Your Painful Past*. Have a journal or notebook, a separate blank piece of paper, and a pen available to write about your journey. You may light some candles and play some soft meditation music to create a warm and relaxing atmosphere.

In this process, you will think of someone who has hurt you. We will invite this person or people to come into our **Sanctuary** and release the energetic, emotional cords keeping us tethered to them.

Start by recalling the hurtful situation and those involved. Try not to get emotionally involved with the story. We want to stay focused on healing not being re-triggered by the past.

Write the story of what you experienced and how it affected you on the separate sheet of paper. Then set this story aside for now.

Begin with the *Journey to Your Sanctuary* meditation from Chapter 1.

When you feel safe and relaxed, imagine a place within your **Sanctuary** where you can invite the person or people you are still struggling with.

Sense them standing in front of you. Feel or imagine an energetic cord connected from your body to their body. You may see or sense a color or texture in this cord. Where does it connect? What does it look like? What does the cord represent to you? Inability to forgive? Heartache? Confusion? Anger? Fear?

Now, you're going to disconnect the cord from your body.

You can imagine a big, thick cord attached to you, draining you emotionally and keeping you controlled by the pain it causes. Visualize and feel yourself being strong and determined, detaching this cord, and sending it back to the person. Feel the autonomy and personal strength as you take your power back. You can say to them, "I take my power back now and release the pain you caused from my life. I am no longer allowing this hurt to affect how I feel. I release you and I forgive you." Take a deep breath in and hold the fullness in your lungs for a moment before releasing it through your mouth. Empty all the emotion you've been holding around this hurt. Again, take a deep breath, gathering up all the emotions, thoughts, and hurt and feel it as you hold your breath for a moment, then with force, exhale through your mouth, pushing out and releasing this energy. You can stay with the breath for a few moments, gathering and releasing as you stay aware of the disconnection of this cord.

Invite a pure white ray of light to come in and fill the space where the cord was attached. Imagine the healing as a ray of light and love fills you, clearing and purifying, until your whole being is filled with beautiful luminous light, glowing within and without.

You can do this process until each person is released.

Stay with this feeling for a few minutes. If the emotional attachment comes back or doesn't feel complete, repeat the process until you feel clear.

When you feel ready, return to your heart center and rest here, breathe deeply and gently move your fingers and toes before opening your eyes.

Journal about your experience, what you saw or sensed, who was involved, and any insight you gained. Write about what you experienced and how you are feeling afterward. When you are finished, tear up the story you wrote of the wounding that you have been carrying and throw it away or burn it. Promise yourself not to forget you have released this and you have taken your power back.

PROCESS
REWRITING THE SCRIPT, REWIRING THE RESPONSE

Begin by thinking about something that usually triggers you.

Write down what emotion or reaction it brings up for you. What is the message that this trigger evokes?

Do you feel a loss of control?
That you are not being trusted?
That people see you in a bad way?
Do you feel rejected?

Write down what thoughts that feeling creates for you.

Where did that trigger originate?

Can you go back in your life to track the earlier times you felt this way?

Now, go into a relaxing heart-centered meditation from Chapter 1. Set your intention to *rewire* the habitual reaction.

When you are relaxed, imagine a circumstance that triggers you. Notice the way you usually react. What feelings come up? What do you do?

Then, while still in meditation, start over and visualize the way you would prefer to respond when the trigger happens. See yourself in your calmest, most confident self.

How do you feel?

Feel yourself keeping your power, shifting into objective thinking, and taking charge of yourself. Create a new vision and emotional connection to that vision.

How does it feel to choose how you respond?

What are the emotions that come up? Do you feel in charge, empowered, and proud of yourself?

After the meditation ends, write out the answers to the following questions:

What was the new way I chose to respond?
How was it different?
How did it feel?
What can I do to instill this new response when I am triggered?

Why is this preferable to getting trapped in the old reaction?

You have the ability to choose from the highest version of yourself. You can design your experience any way you want.

Now that you have experienced what it can feel like to shift out of reacting, you can practice P.B.R.S. to assist you in this process. When you notice you are reacting to a trigger, PAUSE, BREATHE, REFLECT, then SPEAK!

The answers you just wrote out above are the motivation to create a new neural pathway. Keep them visible and remind yourself often of what you wrote.

MEDITATION
ENERGETIC ANGER RELEASE

Energetic Anger Release is used when anger is stored in the nervous system, thoughts, and emotions. Unresolved anger is like a poison eating away at our well-being and happiness. Often, this repressed anger will burst out, unexpectedly causing havoc in our lives. Consciously releasing anger is a powerful way to shift from **React to Respond.**

Begin with a *Journey to Your Sanctuary* to relax the body and mind.

- Notice where in your body you are holding anger, old or new. Does it have a color or texture?
- Are you remembering a specific situation that left you angry?
- Notice the anger without getting attached to the emotions and thoughts around it. Step into the observer role. Imagine a ball of energy building in your heart center; this is a ball of healing and clearing.

- Visualize this ball moving throughout your whole body, down your torso, down and back up each leg, moving up the back and spine, up to the head, into the mind and down your face and neck, down each arm, and through your chest, lungs, and stomach.

As this ball moves throughout your body, it is cleaning and clearing all the anger you have stored in your body, nervous system, and mind. Imagine what color it becomes as it attracts and gathers all the anger you are holding.

When you have cleared as much of what is ready to be released today, take a deep breath in through your nose, hold it and imagine the ball filled with all this anger gathering in your lungs. Release it through your mouth with intention and force, emptying your lungs and belly completely.

Do this release three times. Gather all the energy held in the ball into your lungs, inhale deeply, hold and then release forcefully through the mouth.

Pause and feel the body, emotions, and mind for a moment. Then imagine again the heart center now filling with beautiful violet light. Feel this healing light overflowing from the heart to all parts of the body and emotions, and filling the thoughts and mind with peace, healing, and transformation.

Rest here in the arms of the healing violet light filling your whole being.

Write in your journal about your experience.

CHAPTER 4

Thoughts Have Power!

"You have the power to change your thoughts and your thoughts have the power to change your life."
—RON WILLINGHAM

PART 1
Phoenix

Thoughts, on their own, don't have power over us. It's the belief we attach to them that gives them power.

MANY STUDIES HAVE SHOWN that our thoughts create an energy field that affects the physical world. Author and scientist, Dr. Masaru Emoto, conducted an experiment using jars of water with words taped on the outside. Some words were positive like *love, appreciation, and thank you.* Some were negative like *hate, Hitler, and war.* The results showed the molecular structure of the water stamped with positive words was far more symmetrical and aesthetically pleasing than the molecular structure of the water from jars with dark, negative phrases. Imagine how this affects our bodies and emotions since our bodies are 60% water!

Thoughts have power! In fact, our thoughts shape and color every one of our experiences and situations. And most of the time we are not even aware this is happening.

Situations are simply that: situations. For example, if I am driving to the store to buy some groceries and another driver pulls out in front of me and I almost hit them, I might think, "What a jerk! They were probably texting and not paying attention. It's so aggravating that people nowadays are paying so much attention to their phones and not driving! I am so sick of cell phones. What happened to just living and being present?" Then I go off into the store and now I am grumpy because of what happened. My whole experience in the store will probably be less enjoyable than it could have been because of what happened on my way there.

Now let's examine what happened. The facts are someone pulled out in front of me, and I almost hit them. Any thoughts I choose to add on to the facts are my choice. They are the feelings I choose to place on the facts. It is the story I am choosing to tell myself about the facts. And this story will determine how I feel.

If in that same situation, my immediate thought was "Yikes! Someone just cut me off! That was scary!" and then I felt thankful I did not hit them or have any accident at all, my mood would be completely different. And yes, you might be thinking, "easier said than done" and you would be right.

We are accustomed to believing we do not have control over our thoughts, and you would be partially correct about that. We can't control the automatic or intrusive thoughts that pop into our heads. However, we can control what we do with them after they pop in. Once we notice where our thoughts are taking us, and the story that follows, we then have a choice. When I notice that I am feeling scared that I had a near-accident and almost hit someone, I can choose where my mind wants to go after that. Our habit would have us believe we don't have control over it. And the mind likes to hang out in the negative. The truth is we can shift out of that old pattern and create whatever story we want around any situation to improve the way we feel and the way we see the world.

The voice inside your head is always talking. It is constantly judging, "this is good" or "this is bad," "you are stupid" or "you did a good job," or other value judgments. When we pay attention to what this inner voice is saying to us, many times it is quite disturbing. Imagine for a second this voice is your roommate. Would you ever want a roommate like that?

Someone who speaks to you the way the voice inside your head does? You would certainly find a new roommate and be horrified someone even thought they could talk to you that way! So why do we do this to ourselves, all day long?

It is because we don't even recognize we are doing it, or worse – perhaps we believe the negative things our inner voice is saying about us.

Let's go back to the story about being cut off on the road and going to the store. If I had chosen more grateful thoughts after being cut off, my mood and my experience at the store would probably have been so much better. And that tone would be set for my day. It would take just a little observation, awareness, and then effort, to direct my mind where I want it to go.

If my goal is to feel happier, calmer, and love myself more, isn't it worth that effort?

This chapter teaches us we can choose to change the limiting thoughts and beliefs we've been holding onto. We do this through noticing what we are thinking and telling ourselves and how it has been conditioned by our circumstances.

This work will enable us to heal the wounding that created the destructive thoughts to begin with. From a healed place, we can create a new story for ourselves. This is a story *we* choose. And this story will come from our deep inner yearning for self-love and wholeness.

PART 2
Scarlett

GOING DEEPER AND PUTTING *THOUGHTS HAVE POWER* INTO PRACTICE

CAN A CONSTRICTIVE THOUGHT create an expansive emotion? How can you tell the difference between expansive and constrictive emotions? Constrictive thoughts feel heavy, discouraging, and contracting. They tell us that we can't, that things won't work out, that life is hard, it's too much work: you know those messages! When we pay attention to these thoughts, we can feel our energy and emotions tightening and contracting. Our creativity and enthusiasm get sucked out and we're left with a void of discouragement. This can leave us feeling alone and victimized.

Expansive thoughts feel spacious, open, uplifting, creative, and exciting. They give us energy and enthusiasm to feel our best and do our best. We may seek out others who have the same feelings and thoughts to share our energy. We feel supported by life and open to good things.

Can you think of examples of each from your own life? What makes each thought expansive or constrictive?

What do you feel when you think these two different types of thoughts?

Here are some examples of both expansive and constrictive thoughts; notice what emotion each statement generates in you.

- Today is a great day!
- Today stinks!
- I'm a loser.
- I'm doing the best I can and it's enough.
- Life is hard.
- No one loves me.
- I'm a good daughter/son, sister/brother, husband/wife, friend.
- I'm smart.
- I have nothing to live for.
- My friends support me.
- I'm healthy and strong.
- I'm not good enough.

Now, in your journal, write some of your own:

Thoughts: Emotions Generated:

As you examine the different emotions, ask yourself:

- What emotions do I prefer to feel?
- What emotions do I prefer not to feel?
- Which emotions do I have the most of?
- What do I think about that creates those feelings?
- How do those feelings affect my mood, what I accomplish, and how I behave?
- And how do I act and react in various situations based on these emotions?

PROCESS
LETTER OF SUPPORT AND ENCOURAGEMENT TO YOURSELF

Often, when our negativity bias takes hold, it's challenging and sometimes impossible to find any positivity to pull ourselves out of the darkness.

For this exercise, we are going to write a letter of love, encouragement, and strength for when we are feeling lost, dark, or trapped in negativity. You can write from what you experienced in your *I AM* journey, reminding yourself of your strengths. What would you say to a friend who is feeling down? Write this with compassion and kindness for yourself and what you are experiencing.

You will need paper and an envelope. If you have markers or colored pens, you can write and decorate your letter with bright, happy drawings and writings. Take some time with this exercise to allow this letter to send you a message of encouragement and kindness when you need it most, reminding you of who you are.

How does it feel to read this? What emotions does it evoke? When you are feeling down, do you think this will remind you that it won't last forever?

Every emotion comes and goes. Like a rolling ball, sometimes we are on top and sometimes we are on the bottom. No emotion stays the same. When we are feeling dark or discouraged, we need support to get through it. This letter helps break the cycle of self-criticism, self-loathing, hopelessness, and despair. This is a way we can give ourselves support and love and understanding. Keep this letter in a place where you can read it whenever you are feeling the need for a pick-me-up.

Remember, **Thoughts, on their own, don't have power over us. It's the belief we attach to them that gives them power.**

We've been learning we can choose to change the limiting thoughts and beliefs we've been holding onto. Our minds are conditioned to go to the negative, a protective mechanism designed to keep us safe. Once we are aware of this, we can take charge of it and create new ways of thinking, feeling, and living.

We do this by noticing our mind and where our past circumstances have been conditioned to go. This will open the possibility of healing the wounding that originally produced our constrictive thoughts. From a healed place, we can create a new story for ourselves. A story *we* choose. As Phoenix says, "This story will come from our deep inner yearning for self-love and wholeness."

PROCESS
TALKING TO OUR CRITICAL VOICE

Often, our critical voice or Bully Voice is so loud we can't hear anything else. It can keep us trapped in negative, limiting thoughts and beliefs. The voice can feel like a tyrant, a tormenter in our brain, constantly putting us down and keeping us from loving ourselves and moving forward in our lives.

Why is the negative so much easier to believe than the positive?

In this exercise, we're going to talk to our own inner Bully, explore why it's there and how to let it go.

Imagine being in a quiet, peaceful place where you can relax. Here, we're going to meet our bully self. You can see yourself in a mirror or imagine looking at this version of yourself.

We'll call these two parts **Bully Voice (BV)** and **True You (TY)**. This reinforces that *we* are not our thoughts and don't have to listen to thoughts that we choose not to.

TY—Hello Bully Voice. I've come today to listen to you and try to understand why you are in my head. It's very hard to feel confident and happy when you are judging me and everything I do. I feel like I can never please you or be enough. This causes me a lot of anxiety and self-doubt.

Feel free to say anything that more exactly fits your story here. Notice what sensations come up in your body, and where they occur, when you say these thoughts to yourself.

BV—I'm here to protect you from getting into trouble. My voice is a warning to keep you safe so you can avoid making mistakes and getting hurt or criticized by others.

TY—That makes sense. I understand your concern. But your criticism makes me feel afraid that I'm not enough, that I won't be able to succeed or achieve my desires in my life. You are holding me back.

Imagine your **BV** speaking this way to a child, or even imagine yourself as that child. Hear the harshness and meanness of your **BV**, as she speaks to this child. What message is your **BV** sharing? How do her words make you feel? Small and powerless? How does this knowledge make you feel? Do you think this is a healthy way to speak or teach a child? Does harshness like this have a positive result?

BV—I'm here to remind you to stay safe and I need to protect you from being vulnerable. It's not safe. You can't handle yourself. You'll be in danger.

TY—I hear what you are saying. Listening to you has been an old pattern I've gotten used to. But all this criticism isn't moving me forward and isn't making me happy and confident. From now on, I will remember I can question your voice. You are just a thought and I have a choice to listen to you or not. I am in charge of myself, and I won't allow you to keep me small anymore.

I am calm and centered. I trust myself. I choose the thoughts that make me feel confident, strong, and capable.

I know it's okay to have a critical voice, but I don't have to believe everything you say anymore. Your BV feels so uncomfortable in my body and my mind. I know your words, your messages, and your point of view, are not true. You are just an over-amplified warning voice. And it causes me too much stress and discomfort.

BV—But what will you do without me to warn you of everything that could go wrong?

TY—I will trust my ability to think and choose from a place of calm and groundedness. I may make some mistakes, but I am safe, and I am in charge. I choose to feel relaxed and confident now. I'm creating a new conversation with my positive voice that will give me guidance and confidence.

Take a moment to allow this to integrate. Notice how your body is feeling.

Write a new dialog with the **Positive Voice**. Practice speaking to yourself from this new **PV**.

PROCESS
BUILDING SELF-ESTEEM

The focus of this exercise is to show how each of us has value and worth, at every stage of our development. While you are building your strengths, you have qualities that are valuable now. You can connect with your self-esteem and feel good about yourself, helping to relieve the critical, judgmental mind that is so damaging to your self-love and self-worth.

Begin by defining:

What is self-esteem, what is self-worth?

What do these terms mean to you, personally? Give examples.

Write on a beautiful piece of paper or in your journal in what ways, and in what circumstances, do you already feel self-esteem.

Think of qualities you feel proud of or good about in yourself. For example, *I'm a good friend, I'm forgiving, I'm a good listener; people can talk to me about their problems, I'm smart.* Take a few minutes to dig deep and find where you feel good about yourself, where you feel worth or value.

When you are finished, hold your paper or journal to your heart; close or lower your eyes and feel into what you wrote. Imagine seeing yourself knowing these things about yourself and feeling proud and full. Embody them; then say to yourself, **I claim and embrace my self-esteem because I am...** (speak each aspect of yourself out loud). Give yourself permission to relax and enjoy feeling good about yourself.

When you are ready, in your journal, answer these questions.

Where and how does embracing my self-esteem add value in my life?

Where and how will my embracing my self-esteem add value to the people in my life—my family, my friends, my coworkers, and the people I meet and deal with?

How can I use my value to support others who are struggling?

Keep this where you can see it and remind yourself:

I Am Valuable!

CHAPTER 5

Understanding the Mind

*"If you do not monitor the stories you
plant in your head, you will get lost amongst the
weeds of your thoughts."*
—SEPI TAJIMA

PART 1
Phoenix

Have you ever thought about thoughts? I've always thought schools should offer a course on "How the Brain and Your Mind Work" every year. This way we can learn how we can program our brains ourselves. Once computers became popular, almost everyone was jumping on board with programming. And, as a society, we tend to think it's crucial to have access to a computer device, whether it's a tablet, a cell phone, or a laptop. We buy a device, or often, devices, and then learn how to use them to access the information and content we wish to access.

Isn't it incredible we already have one of these supercomputers in our heads and nobody offers classes to young children on how to properly program it? Once you understand that you can program your mind, you may also wonder, "Why didn't anyone ever teach me this before? This should be taught in schools!"

So, let's look for a moment at what the mind is. Try this experiment. Think of something right now. It can be anything. Now say what you were thinking out loud as if I was sitting there with you and I asked you to tell me what you just thought. You can *observe* the thought that was just in your mind.

Let's look at dogs for a moment. If you let a dog outside and another dog comes and barks and scares him and he runs inside, does he come in and think "Damn! That dog terrified me! I'm such a loser for being so scared! I hate myself!"? No. He comes in, and probably he shakes off the fear and curls up inside to relax and calm down until he feels safe again. He works purely on instinct. He doesn't analyze anything through his thoughts. He *feels* things and acts purely on feeling. That is the difference with humans. We have been given the gift, and the curse, of the ability to analyze and critically think. However, this can mess us up if we don't continuously watch where our minds go.

That being said, if your mind has a thought, and you can observe it, then it is safe to say *you are not your mind.* There is the mind that has thoughts, and then there is the *observer* of those thoughts. Two separate entities. **The Mind** and **The Observer of the Mind.** Now that blows some people's minds when they first hear this!

So, who is the observer? The observer is *YOU*. Your true self. The pure energy and truth of who you are. The part of the mind that is in constant narration is the ego. The ego is defined as *the part of the mind that mediates between the conscious and the unconscious and is responsible for reality testing and a sense of personal identity* (New Oxford American Dictionary).

It is like a computer telling the story of what is happening all around you. When you are very young, your mind is not programmed as fully as it will be, when you get older. When you are born, you are already perfect. Before we get messages to the contrary, we often believe we are the best singer, dancer, or dresser! Some people receive negative messaging right away—as soon as they realize they are a separate self. For others, it takes a few years. For those of you who had a few years of believing you are the best, you were excited to wear your favorite pajamas to school to show your friends. You always wanted to sing and dance for everyone because you knew you were great at it.

And then what happens? Our minds (our inner computers) receive messages and create programs. Maybe our mothers or fathers say, "Be quiet! Nobody wants to hear your singing. It hurts my ears." Or a teacher at school says, "You can't wear your pajamas to school. You're being inappropriate." Suddenly we believe we are not great at singing, and that we are inappropriate. Our minds get programmed with stories other people tell us *about us*. Not from real facts, but from their own opinions. From their own insecurities. From what *they* were programmed to believe from others in their lives. And from there, our minds continue to get programmed by peers, from media, social media, bosses, co-workers, boyfriends/girlfriends, family, spouses, and so on and so on.

Let's return to the story of the Golden Buddha in the introduction to this book. These messages are like clumps of mud getting stuck on to us. *You are not smart enough. You are not pretty because you don't look like this. You are not good enough. You are different. You are weird. You are too sensitive. You are too quiet. You are too loud. You can't do this because you aren't talented enough or smart enough. Why can't you be more like your sister, your brother, and the other kids at school?* And it goes on and on over the years until we are so covered up by the stories other people have told us of who we are; we forget who we are because our true self is so hidden under all the mud.

And then we feel anxiety and depression and wonder why. It takes a lot of energy to live up to those expectations and try to fit into who others want us to be. Many people will want you to be many different things. And that is exhausting. Ultimately you are "faking it" if your behavior doesn't align with who you truly are, and ultimately leaves us feeling anxious and/or depressed.

If at this point you are nodding your head and thinking, "Yes, that's me. I totally understand this," you are not alone. And that is where the title of this book comes in—***You Are Already Perfect, You Just Forgot***. This work is not about fixing yourself. It's about finding yourself. All the stories and messages you were told before will now need to be challenged to see if they are true about who you are. And if they are not the truth of who you are, then they must gently be undone. Underneath all the crap you have believed for so long is a beautiful, perfect person waiting to emerge and live an incredible life. This person is the *observer* of the mind. Once we understand this, we can start the sweet work of changing how we think. We realize we can choose the thoughts that reflect the true story of who we are.

The first step in this process is to take a day or two and pay attention to your thoughts—what your mind dwells on, where your thoughts tend to lead you. And take notes on what you notice: keep a small notebook with you or make notes on your phone. Notice when you are feeling anxious and write down what you are thinking at that moment. What about when you are feeling depressed—what is going through your mind then? When a mood hits, observe the mind. What is it talking about? And also—when you are feeling calm and happy, what is the mind doing then? This is very important because it will give you a window into the computer programming in the mind. Once we can see how it is programmed, we can uninstall any viruses corrupting it.

PART 2

Scarlett

GOING DEEPER AND PUTTING *UNDERSTANDING THE MIND* INTO PRACTICE

WHATEVER WE'VE BEEN CONDITIONED to believe comes from our early messages from family, school, religion, society, and so on. Psychologists tell us most of our personalities and our beliefs about life are formed by the time we are seven years old!

Many of us keep perpetuating the same belief systems generation after generation. We believe what our parents believed about us; we think of ourselves the way our young minds perceived those around us thinking about us.

Some of these messages may be positive or expansive and some may be negative, or constrictive. In many cases, it's a mixed message. As children, we unconsciously mold ourselves based on what we see around us. Often, our models show us what is possible for us. And sometimes, what isn't possible.

In Chapter 4, we learned, *Thoughts, on their own, don't have power over us. It's the belief we attach to them that gives them power.*

We're going to deepen the practice of knowing and trusting ourselves. We're continuing to reframe what we've been conditioned to believe about ourselves and what the possibilities are for our life based on those beliefs. We're introducing the practice of **Who Said?** as a way to disengage from the familiar pattern of giving your power and choice away. Here, the conditioning that causes deep wounding and beliefs around shame, hopelessness, not feeling good enough, and beliefs that good things are only for others, not for me, are revealed and exposed for the "mud" they are. You will see how these old programs or beliefs limit your happiness, success, love, and freedom to create the life you yearn for and how to take charge of them.

We've been working with noticing our thoughts and understanding our mind's reactive negativity bias. Fear and insecurity are very powerful forces when we're faced with choices. The brain's fear center wants to keep us safe; to do that, it will subconsciously steer us away from taking a chance. When we become more familiar with the brain's patterns, we can notice what's influencing us, measure the risk, and make a conscious choice about what's best for us.

Our thoughts create our feelings.

Our feelings directly affect our choices.

Our choices create our circumstances.

With this powerful knowledge, we become aware we're engaging in old thought patterns. We can pause, step into the observer position, and literally ask our mind, *Who Said?* We confront the thought and ask it to prove itself. *Are you based on facts, or did someone tell you this?*

When you have a limiting or negative thought, pause, and ask:

Who said? Who told me this was true?

Who made me believe this is the way I am or the way things have to be for me?

Try to track back to earlier times in your life when you had this thought or belief and question the source of it. Ask yourself, *Is that true for me or am I holding onto someone else's story? Who told me that or made me think that way? What belief system were they operating from?*

An example of this in my life is when I got my Doctor of Naturopathy degree. I called my mom to tell her we have a doctor in the family! Her response was not what I was expecting. She reacted from her own fear that subconsciously shaped me as a child. She said to me, "Don't tell anyone. They'll ask you questions, and you won't know the answers."

Although this was hurtful and devastating to me at the time, I later realized my mother was trying to protect me from what she feared. She was speaking from the voice of her negativity bias. She projected onto me her fear and experiences of feeling embarrassed. This reflected and reinforced my early fear of speaking which began with my second-grade Catholic school experience of shame that shaped my self-esteem and confidence.

This was a circumstantial and generational wounding I had to heal so I didn't continue to live from it and unconsciously pass it down to my daughter. It had become my belief, because of others' opinions, not my own.

As we question the beliefs limiting us, we take our power back by choosing our own truth. For example:

- When a person or a circumstance is making you feel bad about yourself (sending a constrictive message) do you have to believe them?
- Do you tend to think they're right and you're wrong?
- What makes their opinion better or more true than yours? Is anyone forcing you to believe them?
- Do you tend to believe and trust other people's opinions over your own? When we do this, we stay stuck in the constrictive beliefs to which we've been conditioned.

Remember, our thoughts create the emotions that influence the choices we make. If you are wondering about the quality of your thoughts, notice the emotion that goes with them. You can ask yourself, *Is this thought making me feel happy, expanded, positive? Or contracted, limited, negative?*

At that moment, you have the power of choice. Your thoughts are your own. If you don't like a thought you're thinking, you have the power to change it. Notice where you hold self-judgment, the feeling of not being enough. It may be a belief you aren't smart enough, attractive enough, or successful enough.

Where did you hear this in your life? Where did this belief come from? Do you have to hold onto this belief? What circumstances, influences, or people can you avoid or limit your exposure to once you identify them as a constrictive influence.

If these constrictive messages are coming from sources like work, school, or family, you may not be able to eliminate being around them, however, you can filter the influence they have.

These are the times to engage the **Who Said?** Process. Sometimes, when we ask **Who Said?** we can hear the voice of the person or situation that shaped our belief, like in the example of my mom.

As I studied and began to understand human behavior, I realized she was suffering from her own conditioned negative beliefs learned from her family dynamic and projecting that onto me. Still, it wasn't mine, it was hers. So, with this knowledge, I had the power to choose. I could continue listening to the voices from long ago limiting my happiness, or I could heal and let go of these childhood programs. I could reclaim the truth that I'm a beautiful, smart, lovable human being!

Everything is an opinion, and you can own yours completely.

> *If you think constrictive thoughts, you will only get constrictive results. If you think expansive thoughts, you will create expansive results.*

For example, you can think, it's not worth doing well in school, I'm not going to college anyway. Or you can think, I'm going to do the best I can in school to prepare for whatever is next.

Whichever statement you choose, you get to be right. If you choose to think life stinks or nothing ever works out for me, you get to be right, your life will stink. If you choose to think life is challenging and exciting, you also get to be right. You will be excited by the challenges coming your way and you'll look for creative solutions.

No one can force you to think or feel anything you don't want to.

You may not have control over your circumstances, however, with practice, you can take charge of what you think and therefore what you feel and experience.

Your thoughts are your own. You can accept or reject any thought that comes into your mind.

- What is an example of a constrictive thought that you commonly have?
- What emotion does it create?

Now, turn it around into an expansive or at least a neutral thought and notice the feeling this creates. Can you see how your thoughts have a direct effect on your moods? How likely is it you will make a good, expansive decision if you feel sad, depressed, angry, or stressed out?

This process of turning the **C** (constrictive) into an **E** (expansive) or neutral thought is so powerful. Because…

Who said?!

What makes "them" right?

Who gives "them" power over you and the way you feel?

Ask this out loud with emphasis and power: ***Who said?!*** whenever you notice a **C** thought and turn it around.

Use this affirmation: *I am in charge of what I think and how I feel. I only allow expansive thoughts to affect how I feel about myself and the choices I make for my life.*

Clearing and healing old limiting beliefs to create a life we're envisioning for ourselves is a two-part process.

First, we uncover where the limiting beliefs originated from by utilizing the *Who Said?* process. Next, we look for examples of the opposite of the limiting thought. For example, I realized my fear and limiting belief around speaking was my mom's fear. Now I could identify Who Said? (my mom) and look for other times when I did speak, and it was comfortable and relaxed. As I opened to this possibility, I found some memories of when I spoke, and it was okay. Now, I have the power of choice. I'm free to make my own decision of how to hold this old belief. When we release this belief, saying, "This is not my story, I'm not bound by believing this way" we reinforce the positive memories and thought processes from when we had a different experience. Even if you can only remember one time, that's enough to rewire our beliefs.

Take a moment to connect to a limiting thought or feeling. Use the *Who Said?* process to track back to where this may have originated. Don't worry if you can't remember exactly who was involved or what the original circumstance was. Just use the questions to distill down the belief.

Then, think back to an experience of feeling the opposite, even if it's a small example. Bring it to the surface of your memory and feel the emotion of it. Allow it to grow in your consciousness and become a visceral feeling in your body, emotions, and thoughts. This creates our new neural pathway we are deepening and choosing to live from.

End this piece by creating a statement describing and acknowledging this positive memory. For me, it was, "I am a powerful and confident speaker. I am comfortable sharing with others." I repeated this statement as I visualized myself speaking comfortably.

PROCESS
SHORT JOURNEY

Visualize yourself standing in your confidence and power as you deflect any constrictive influence. Like a superpower, your choice of what to think is your shield and sword. When we visualize a new way of behaving, it sends a message to our subconscious about how we want it to behave. By reinforcing this frequently, we create a new story for the brain. We can access an expansive story for ourselves.

MEDITATION
LAY DOWN YOUR BURDENS

Begin with a shortened version of the **Journey to Your Sanctuary** from Chapter 1. As you relax into your **Sanctuary** and are exploring your landscape, you notice your back is feeling tired and achy. You realize you are carrying a heavy backpack you hadn't noticed before.

In your landscape, take the backpack off and place it in front of you on the ground. Opening it, you see it is filled with large rocks. Each rock represents a hurtful voice, limiting belief, wounding, lack of forgiveness, resentment, or heartache you've been carrying inside.

One by one, take out each rock. Hold it in your hands and see what each one represents to you. Anger, rejection, inadequacy, victimhood, shame, abuse, not feeling protected. Or?

As you hold each rock in your hands, allow all the feelings inside of you to transfer to this rock, and then set the rock down on the earth with compassion and gentleness for what you've been holding inside. Take all the time you need and imagine the rock melting into the earth until it has completely disappeared.

Continue with each rock until the backpack is empty. Then stand up, turn your face up to the sky and receive a beautiful beam of white light flowing into your heart. As you walk back to your Sanctuary gate, notice how you are feeling and if your landscape has changed.

Journal about what you released. Create your new story of how your life will feel without these old burdens. Connect to the expansive possibilities for your life without these burdens weighing you down.

CHAPTER 6

The Truth of Who You Are

"Your time is limited, so don't waste it living someone else's life. Don't be trapped by dogma—which is living with the results of other people's thinking. Don't let the noise of others' opinions drown out your own inner voice. And most important, have the courage to follow your heart and intuition."
—STEVE JOBS

PART 1
Phoenix

So how was it observing your mind? Did anything surprise you? If you are anything like me, or most humans, you are probably saying you are surprised how much time you spend beating yourself up or saying mean things to yourself. We all know we do it. I never realized how much my inner self-talk colors everything I do until I started paying attention to my thinking, instead of just letting my thoughts run as they would. It's as though we can't be in the present moment because we are too busy analyzing the present moment. And for the most part, the analysis is negative. How can we enjoy anything we do when there is a constant critic riding along on our journey with us?

Have you ever taken a trip or gone out to dinner with someone who was in a bad mood? How was that experience? My guess is, not so great. Our mind is like the crabby companion, except we take it everywhere. It constantly speaks to us in a critical, negative way, so of course, we feel anxious and depressed.

Now, you may be thinking, but what if my mind is right about me? What if I am those qualities my mind says I am? I couldn't have made them up, right? I do feel as if I'm stupid. I do feel ugly.

In this part of the book, we will examine the things your mind has been programmed to think, to see if those things are true. Maybe it is time for an update, a reset of your own truth. Because if these are the things creating anxiety and depression for you, and you want to "be happy," then it is time to start reprogramming the old mind computer.

I am going to give you an example of how this worked for me and the amazing outcome I experienced. I was working in a high school in Newark, NJ. I was also doing private-practice counseling after work. Parking in the Ironbound section of Newark, where my school was located, is notoriously difficult. On this particular day, I unintentionally parked my car so it was blocking someone's driveway. I am a very conscientious parker and would never want to block someone in and make their life difficult. And I do not particularly like getting my car towed. As I said, I had not intentionally parked this way—the driveway had an extension that looked almost like a patio, which is what I was blocking.

I came out of work and headed towards my car, in a bit of a rush since I had a private-practice appointment right after school. The appointment was with a 19-year-old girl we will call Angela. Angela was suffering from anxiety and depression. She felt stupid and ugly and worthless. She was in college and miserable. Unfortunately, Angela grew up with a cruel, abusive father who was always telling her how stupid she was. One day, she found him cheating on her mother in her parents' bedroom. He became crueler after that, saying she was ugly and worthless. Eventually, her mother left her father and Angela lived with her mother and older brother.

But things did not get any better for Angela. Her mother was a very anxious person, not certain how she was going to support herself and her children, and nothing Angela did was ever right or good enough. Angela was young, and no matter how hard she tried to do her best, she could not please anyone. Her older brother followed in her father's footsteps, and the emotional abuse continued. Now, at age 19, Angela continued to believe she was ugly, stupid, and worthless; she had never learned how to be happy. Does any part of this story ring true for you?

Back to the story about my car. As I approached it before my session with Angela (no, thankfully I did not get towed!), I noticed a yellow Post-it note on my driver's side window. I peeled it off and read,

"You are just another STUPID person, blocking my driveway. Next time I will have you towed!"

A pit opened up in my stomach after reading those words. They felt so mean and angry. They were so nasty, and I honestly hadn't meant to block their driveway. I crumpled up the note, intending to throw it out later. With my hands, I brushed off the negative energy I felt on my body. I literally brushed it off as if there were crumbs all over me, which I do when I feel someone's negative energy on me.

I got in my car and started to drive to my session. I was thinking about the message on the Post-it note and the messages Angela had gotten about herself from her father and brother. I realized—we are born perfect. In the previous chapter I talked about how, when we are little, we believe we are perfect until the negative messages start pouring in, telling us we are *helpless, unlovable, worthless, in danger (because the world is a dangerous place)*. Faced with others' opinions, we not only forget the perfect person we are but create a new belief system based on those opinions.

I uncrumpled the Post-it note telling me I was stupid. I realized the messages Angela had heard her whole life were different Post-its stuck on her. There were so many: "You are stupid," "You are ugly," "You are worthless," "You are such a bitch," "Why were you born anyway?" "I shouldn't have had children," and finally, "*YOU ARE UNLOVABLE.*"

Eventually, you look down and see yourself so covered in these notes that you fully and unquestioningly believe their messages. I reflected on the way the Post-its were like the mud covering the Golden Buddha. You believe the messages are the truth of who you are. All you can see are the notes, or the mud because they have covered over the real you for so long. You can't see any other version of yourself, and you don't even know the notes are there. You feel like the covered-up you *is* the real you.

The truth of who you are is underneath those messages: the perfection of that baby born into this world, absolutely perfect. The one who could sing and dance freely without the worry of being judged. The one who could wear pajamas to school and feel absolutely beautiful. So, as we said in the subtitle of this book, "it's not about fixing yourself, it's about finding yourself." Meaning, that we have to peel off and examine each Post-it note, each message, to see if it is true.

When I had my session with Angela, I told her about the note I'd found on my car and all it had made me realize. Then we wrote down on a Post-it, *"You are stupid."* I asked her to stick it on her shirt. She did. We then took all of her beliefs—*I am ugly, I am a bitch, I am worthless, I am unlovable*—wrote them on individual Post-its, and stuck them all over her body, face, and head. She looked in the mirror and started to cry. She was able to see on the outside what she had been feeling on the inside. It was enormously powerful.

I asked her how it made her feel to wear the negative messages. She said horrible. I then asked her if we could examine the truth of each statement. And she agreed. We came up with two lists: facts supporting the assumption that she is stupid and facts supporting the assumption that she is smart. Then we examined what *stupid* means. How do you know someone is stupid? Can a stupid person get accepted by a college? Can a stupid person graduate from high school? Do tests determine stupidity? Can you be smart and not be good at taking tests? Is academia the sole determination of smart or stupid? Is it possible to have a third-grade education and still be smart? And on and on we went. And in the end, there were *no facts* to support the belief that she was stupid.

So, I asked, "What is the truth then?" And she said, "I think I am actually smart." I wrote that truth on a brighter Post-it, then asked her to peel off the "You are stupid" note and replace it with the one that said, "I think I am actually smart." I asked her how wearing the new note made her feel. She said she felt great: "A little uncomfortable but good!"

The discomfort comes with getting used to a new truth. Breaking old habits can feel uncomfortable, but with time and practice, old habits will die, and the new habits will feel comfortable and natural. I asked her which truth she wanted to wear from now on, and she said without hesitation, "I think I am actually smart." And then she said that she could see how in the near future she'd want to change it to "I am smart." She wanted to wear the first truth for a little while, and when she felt comfortable with it, go on to the next one. We examined how she had come to believe she was stupid: what messages she had gotten at school or from her peers and family members. She began to realize that the messages, even though they'd been spoken, weren't necessarily true. Other truths were possible. In Scarlett's next chapter, you will find the ***Post-It Note Exercise*** written out for you to follow.

In the following chapters, we will learn how to start incorporating these new truths into our lives and how to grow new neural pathways in our minds that will lead us to happier, more fulfilling lives.

PART 2
Scarlett

GOING DEEPER AND PUTTING *THE TRUTH OF WHO YOU ARE* INTO PRACTICE

BEFORE WE MOVE FORWARD, I invite you to consider what you've learned so far. In your journal, or on a piece of paper, take a moment to answer these questions:

How has this work affected me so far?
What have I gained and realized?
What has stood out for me the most?
In what ways am I implementing these things into my daily life?

When I was completing my shamanic training and initiation, my teacher told me that if I didn't "grow corn" with what I was experiencing and learning, it was just fancy information to share at cocktail parties. If we don't take the information we are given and transform it into personal knowledge, there is no power or healing available from that information. It is just data…

Metabolizing the information available to us from what we learn, and experience is the alchemical process of transforming straw into gold, pain into possibilities, and wounds into wisdom.

In the past modules we've been learning we all have choices about what we believe. In this chapter, we will go deeper into envisioning what our lives could be by releasing our conditioned beliefs. These practices will take us deeper into healing and disconnecting from our old stories of wounding and limitation. Then we can open up to the highest version of ourselves.

We'll begin with the *Post-It Note Exercise* developed by Phoenix.

PROCESS
POST IT NOTE

- First, write out all of the beliefs you have about yourself on Post-it notes, using the words "*I am* _____." Now put them all over your body and look in the mirror. Reflect on how you feel, looking at yourself with all the beliefs you have about yourself stuck all over you.
- Next, take out two pieces of paper. On the top of one piece write *Old Story*. Under **Old Story**, write Chapters 0 to your current age. (I am currently 53 so my page would have OLD STORY: 0–53.) Each chapter represents a year of your life.
- On top of the other piece of paper write: *New Story*. Under **New Story** write *Chapter 54*, or your current age. Now take off all the Post-it notes you put on your body. Place them all on the **Old Story** paper. Look at all the notes. Are there any you want to continue believing in your **New Story**? Maybe they weren't all negative beliefs. If you have any you don't want to change, move them over to the **New Story** paper.

Now take one of the beliefs from the **Old Story** that you would like to challenge. As I did with Angela, question how true each belief is, based on *facts*, not *feelings*. If you think you are ugly, what is beauty and what is ugly? Are we simply living by others' standards? And does everyone in the world live by the same definition?

In some cultures, being skinny is considered beautiful. You can then go to another country where having some weight on you is a sign of being healthy and beautiful, and where being skinny means you must be ill or unable to feed yourself properly. So, which is true?? Are you ugly or are you beautiful?? It seems to me that you are neither—those are values put on you by your culture. It must mean beauty is subjective and the only opinion that matters is *yours*. Do you want to continue energizing the belief that you are ugly, or is it time to energize a new truth?

If your new truth is now, "*I am beautiful,*" WRITE a NEW Post-it note that says *I am beautiful*. Take the new truth, *I am beautiful*, and place it on the **New Story,** Chapter __ (your current age) paper.

Remember, our life is like a story in the process of being written and you are the main character. Each chapter is a year of your life. If you had a novel and could only read chapters 1 through whatever age you are over and over again, would you want to do that? Or would that get very boring after a while? Your future awaits in the blank pages of this novel, and you can write whatever story you want for your character.

In life, we are always receiving messages from our culture, from other people, which become our personal Post-its and get stuck on us. It is up to us if we want to wear them or not. If we do not want to wear one of those messages and know it immediately, then straight away, we can energetically rip it off and throw it away. We then place our hands over our hearts and energize the story we are choosing for ourselves.

As you create your **New Story,** ridding yourself of your old messages, you can let your Child Self know she will be safe and loved and that Old Story will not be part of who she is anymore.

Practice living your *New Story* all week. Maybe take some action trying on your NEW messages. For example, if you hate your body, each day, place the *New Story* Post-it on yourself and look at yourself in the mirror. Compliment yourself and your body. When you have gotten comfortable with this message from your *New Story,* take another Post-it from your *New Story* and practice wearing that one, and telling yourself *that* message. Continue this process until all of your old, unwanted *I Am* messages are transformed into your new Truths.

Which story do you want to energize?
You are the golden Buddha underneath the old messages.
You are already perfect. YOU JUST FORGOT.

CREATING YOUR NEW STORY

It can be scary to let go of limiting beliefs. We have to step out of our comfort zones and be vulnerable in order to grow. We're like a new seedling, popping out of the safety of the earth, tender and vulnerable. Imagine the discomfort of feeling so tender, not knowing how life is going to be but not being able to stop yourself from growing and trying to reach up to the sun. Your very nature won't allow you to stay in the safety of the earth's warm, dark embrace. You can't deny that absolute pull to grow.

This is when we start the process of creating our map for our lives. We connect with what our hearts yearn to feel and experience, to find the gold under all the mud. What is the feeling state we want? This will be the foundation of the map, the landscape from which we create.

We connect with our feelings rather than thoughts to guide us to our heart's yearning. Feelings help us step out of the trapping of our logical mind and what *makes sense* for us based on our conditions. Some of the external things that dictate how much we believe we can achieve are our gender, our level of education, our family dynamic, our income, or our profession, or degree. Have you ever heard the saying, "What you believe, you will achieve?" Now is the time to expand what we believe so we can expand what we achieve!

Take out your notebook or journal and contemplate these questions. Answer from a place of expansion. Even if your mind argues, take a moment to imagine your life from the landscape of possibility:

- What does my heart yearn to feel?
- What is the reason I want to feel this; what is my "Reason Why?"
- How will living this life feel differently?
- What effect will this new way of living have on me?
- How will the quality of my life improve?

This is a very important piece. Without a strong connection to your *Reason Why* that keeps pulling you forward and keeping you committed, you can easily give up and fall back into limiting patterns and conditioning from your past.

Creating a new story or map of how we want to feel in our lives and having a strong vision for our conscious and subconscious mind to follow, keeps us anchored to our higher possibilities. Without this, we can easily get stuck in the realm of probability where each tomorrow will probably be a lot like yesterday, and each passing year will probably feel a lot like the last year or last decade.

MEDITATION
I AM (REVISITED)

We're going to revisit the *I AM* Journey and combine it with your new story, your story of what's possible for your life. Visualize and feel into your desire on this journey, connecting with your *golden self* and the highest possibilities for your life.

Begin by sitting or lying down comfortably and noticing your breath, the coolness on your nostrils as you inhale, and the warmth on your upper lip as you exhale. With your next exhale, allow your feet and legs to get heavy and to relax. Notice your hips and belly softening and relaxing with each breath. Now, pay attention to your back muscles and your spine relaxing. If there is any tension or tightness in your shoulders and neck, allow it to melt down your arms and out your fingertips. Finally, notice your head relaxing and melting any tension from your forehead and brow. Relax your jaw and allow your teeth to separate as your whole face relaxes. Moving down your throat, into your chest, notice the rise and fall of your inhale and exhale. With no effort, your body is breathing. Notice or imagine the beating of your own heart.

Now, imagine your heart center opening and illuminating a pathway. This is your path of heart, of love, and peace. Sense yourself moving down this pathway, noticing what you see and feel around you on your path of love. At the end of the pathway is a gate. When you are ready, push open the gate and take three steps down 1,2,3, and onto the landscape of your sacred space. Explore what you see and feel around you in this safe, peaceful space. It may be a place you've been before or a brand-new place you are creating now. Take time to explore and feel the love and safety that is around you. What do you see? Feel? Hear? What colors or textures? Fully experience this wonderful, peaceful space and enjoy being here. As you relax more fully, sense any tension or stress you've been carrying just releasing and melting away... as if you're emptying out your body and mind. Each exhale releases stress; each inhale brings in lightness and peace until your whole body and mind are glowing from the light within.

Now, notice someone is walking toward you. They look intriguing and emanate a safe and comfortable feeling.

As they approach, you notice it is you. This is the highest, most fulfilled version of yourself. Take some time to notice what you see, feel, and perceive from this version of yourself.

How do you dress? How do you walk and carry yourself? What feelings, what vibration, are you radiating?

Now, your highest version of yourself takes your hand and leads you to a place where you are living your life of possibilities. This place has all of the aspects of how you yearn to feel, express, and move in your life.

Take some time to notice what you are being shown. What kind of life are you living? Who is in your life, what kind of people, partners? What kind of lifestyle do you have? Are you in nature or the city? What country? What type of work or service are you offering? Does it fulfill you? What is the feeling you notice as you step into this life? What are your qualities, strengths? What traits do you notice? What do you see in your eyes?

Spend a few minutes with this vision of yourself and your life. *Feel* what it's like to be this person in this life. You can ask questions of yourself.

For example:

What can I do now to move me closer to this life?
How can I stay anchored to this yearning, so I may fulfill it?
What do I need to release or resolve to allow this life to

open up?
Is there any wisdom or advice you have for me today?

When you feel complete, allow your highest self to walk you back to the *Sanctuary* gate. If there is anything else you'd like to say or express, take a moment to do this before stepping up the three steps and walking back down the path of heart that brought you here...

Settle back into your heart center, taking as long as you need to gently come back to the body, connecting to the breath.

Take a deep breath, wiggle your fingers and toes, and gently open your eyes.

Take some time to write in your journal all that you experienced.

PROCESS
CREATING A VISION BOARD

Now, we'll create a Vision Board to reflect and anchor what you found.

Take cardboard or foam board and create a Vision or, Goal Board with images, words, and drawings representing the life you yearn to live, the way you want to feel, and the goals you have. You can use any materials you are attracted to—magazines, printed images from the Internet, drawings, stickers, words, and inspirational phrases.

Our subconscious mind, where we create most of what we experience in our lives, speaks in and learns from images and symbols. A Vision (or Goal) Board with strong, powerful images will act as a mental compass to keep feeding the subconscious with fuel to move you in the direction of your true life's highest possibilities.

On the top of the Board, write,

What can I do today to move me closer to my most fulfilling life?

This is very important. Once we have our vision and connection to what we yearn for, we have to actively engage that desire. We have to stay awake and consciously look for opportunities to grow our desires. Who can you talk with to share your vision or find support? Where can you show up and what can you explore that will increase your knowledge about the life you want to create? What research can you do? Where can you be of service to learn more and make connections to help you move in the direction you want to go? These active choices will give you the power to energize your possibilities.

Then write,

What limitations or fears do I need to overcome/heal/reframe so I can move closer to the life that is calling me?

Are there any voices sending you negative messages, telling you this can never happen? If so, recognize these fears and negativity as the conditioned mind. Using the practices you've learned in previous chapters, take charge of these voices by asking *Who Said?!* Release your old limitations and wounding by unhooking from a painful past, or any of the other practices you felt connected to. This is an imperative aspect in the creation of your newly lived life. By energizing your possibilities and your Vision, you can release and heal the limitations that might sabotage your fulfillment.

Create statements and affirmations directly relating to what you are choosing for your life. Paste them on your Vision Board and keep this where you can see it; meditate on it and energize it with your intention and commitment every day. This is your new contract, your commitment to yourself, and the life waiting for you.

The path to your vision may take some time and you may experience some twists and turns along the way. Be patient and continue to trust in yourself as you energize your highest life and use your *"**Reason Why**"* and **Who Said?!** to stay on course.

CHAPTER 7

How to Live by This New Truth

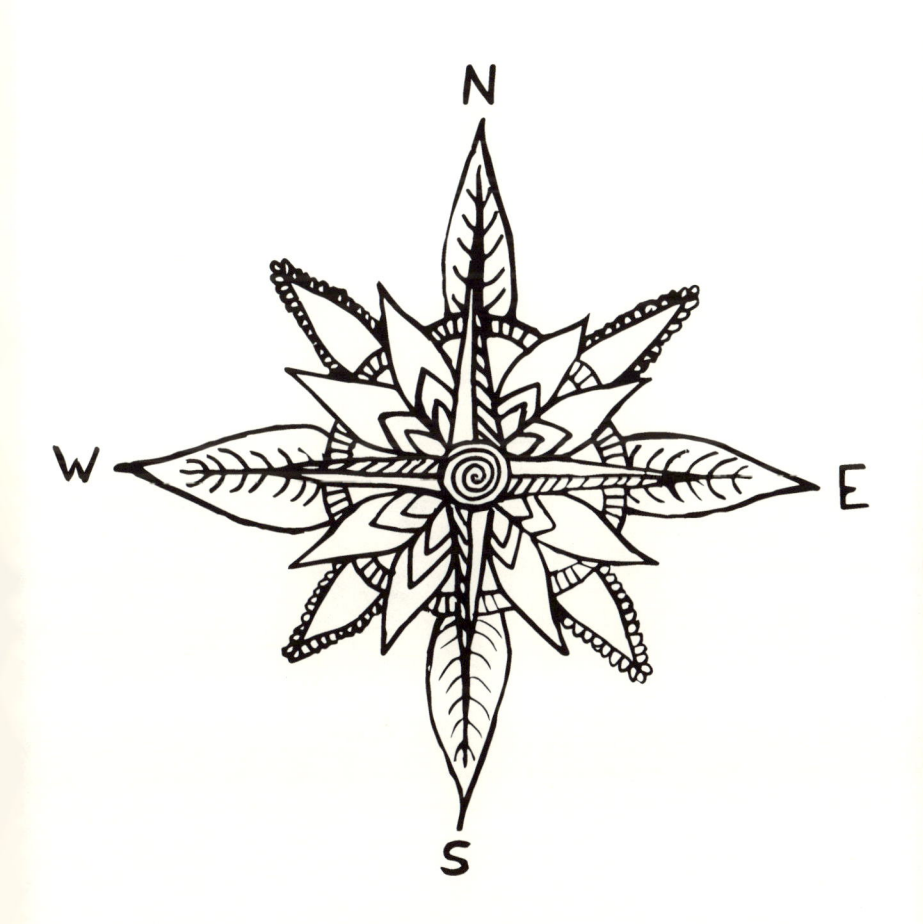

"Confidence is not 'they will like me.' Confidence is 'I'll be fine if they don't.'"
—CHRISTINA GRIMMIE

PART 1
Phoenix

IF YOU HAVE MADE it to this chapter, you have, I hope, begun to realize that many of the things you believed about yourself are, in fact, someone else's opinions. And it is our hope you are challenging some of those "old stories" and are writing some new ones.

In the Post-it exercise, we have you put the old beliefs under **Old Story** and the new beliefs in the *New Story*. As we explained earlier, the reason we do this is to look at your life like chapters in a book. For instance, if I am 24 years old, I have completed 24 years and am in my 25th. If I gave you a book and said, "Please read this book. It has 100 chapters, but you must read Chapters 1–24 over and over again." You would want to know what happens to the main character, right? How does she/he change and grow and what new adventures are they having?

When we continue to retell the same old stories about ourselves, we are reliving our previous chapters over and over. They are written already. They are done, signed, sealed, and delivered, and unless you have invented a time machine where you can go back and change some stuff, it is *over*. What is the point of hanging out there? And if you are choosing to hang out there, how is it making you feel? My guess is, not great since you are reading this book and looking to make some changes in your life.

What if I looked at Chapter 25 as nothing but blank pages? What if I took all the new Post-it notes and wrote my next chapter with those? Now that would be something to read! That is the space where change is possible. You can't place the new notes on the past. It is done. And you can't place them in the future because there is no such thing—it will never be *here*. The only thing we have control of is *The Now*. (Side note: if you haven't read Eckhart Tolle's *The Power of Now*, I highly recommend it.)

This is where we start. Since your mind has become accustomed to the old beliefs, it will take some time to create new habits, but the good news is that it's possible, no matter how old you are! That is where neuroplasticity comes in. Imagine your brain is like a forest. And your habits are like hiking trails. When we go to a mountain for a hike, we go down the trails that are already mapped and flattened out. There are usually signs along the way showing us where to turn and where to go. Once we pick a trail, it often has a color scheme so we can look at the trees and follow the colored trail markers.

Now say, for instance, you got to the mountain and decided to create your own trail. You would have to take your time—cut out the branches, walk down the path, clear the brush. You would need to create some trail markers, so you remembered the direction you were heading in. Eventually, if you kept at it long enough, the old trail would become overgrown with brush and bushes. And the new path would be the one you got used to using. Our brain works the same way. The more we think about and do things in a certain way, the more likely our brain is to create trails—neural pathways—it becomes accustomed to using. When we think in a new way, our brain's habits try to keep us on the old trails because they are familiar. It takes time to remind the mind we are switching over to the new trail. And that is where the trail markers come in.

Think of these trail markers as reminders to yourself that you are blazing a new trail in your mind. When you look in the mirror and your old belief says, "You are ugly," you will need to remind yourself that that is your **Old Story.** That is the *Old Trail*. And it would help to put something on the mirror to point the way to your new trail, such as a Post-it note with your new story on it. Maybe your new story about your appearance is "Beauty is subjective, and who is to say I am not beautiful!" This is a trail marker. Follow this new trail. Because where is the old trail getting you? Depressed? Anxious? Feeling unlovable or unworthy? Is that where you want to be headed?

If the answer is no, then *choose* to go down the new trail. Each time you do, you are creating a new groove in your brain that will eventually get accustomed to your new story. This is science, folks—not just a concept. Neuroplasticity is a real thing. But much like creating a new hiking trail on the mountain, creating a new pathway in your brain takes effort and daily commitment to doing the work: shifting out of the old beliefs, the old story, the previous chapters, and creating and following the new trail markers. You need to have the reminders around you to bring you to your new story. And if you forget and notice you're feeling sad or anxious (let your moods be your markers, too), look into your thoughts. What are you thinking about? I guarantee, *old story* thoughts. When you notice them, shift to your new Post-its, your *new story* thoughts.

There is a quote I love by Lisa M. Hayes: "Be careful how you talk to yourself because you are listening!" Imagine what it would do to another person, but especially a young child, if you said out loud to them what you said to yourself. Every time you talk to yourself, you are talking to that little child inside of you, and you are listening. You believe what you are saying, and it is creating the story of you.

James Allen once said, "You are today where your thoughts have brought you; you will be tomorrow where your thoughts take you." This is a perfect way to sum up the idea that we are the designers of our existence through our minds. Once we see we can change the design, the possibilities for our lives open up. We don't know what we don't know. But now that you know how to start challenging your old beliefs and creating new ones, where do you want to go? What thoughts will you cultivate to take you somewhere new, beautiful, and peaceful?

Have you ever stopped to notice the voice in your head is ALWAYS TALKING? Instead of being fully present to what is happening outside ourselves, our minds are narrating each and every event. It's like having a sports commentator inside our heads. If you stop and listen to this voice, I am guessing you are like the rest of us, that most of what it is saying is not very kind. It is more like a **Bully:**

> "You are so fat and gross."
>
> "Why are you so skinny? You look sick all the time."
>
> "You are so stupid."
>
> "You are so unlovable. You will probably die alone."
>
> "You are worthless. You don't even deserve to live."

And that is to name just a few. It is said we have about 60,000 thoughts a day. I am guessing the majority of them are from the Bully. Think about it. What rings more true? The thoughts I just mentioned or the following:

> "You are so beautiful."
>
> "Your body is so perfect exactly as it is."
>
> "You are so smart and witty. People are lucky to be around you."
>
> "You are so lovable."
>
> "You are valuable. Your life matters."

It's almost hard to read, right? Like, if I think that, I'm conceited or full of myself. This is the programming. This is the way we are taught to think, which is totally absurd. Then we wonder why there's so much depression, anger, and suicide in the world. As we all know, we are conditioned to feel more comfortable with insults than with compliments.

What we want to talk about here is the other voice. The voice of the best friend. This voice is generally neglected, pushed away, dismissed, ignored, or not believed. Even when she tries to speak, we feel that we shouldn't think so highly of ourselves, we shouldn't feel that we are better than anyone else.

Have you ever thought about the term that gets thrown around all the time—*self-centered*? We use it in such a negative manner. In reality, shouldn't we be centered on our selves before branching out to anyone else? How can we feel fulfilled and happy if we feel crappy on the inside and try to give away to others what we are lacking within ourselves? One of my favorite Wayne Dyer thoughts is that you can't give away what you don't have. He says, "What happens when you squeeze an orange? What do you get?" You would reply, "Orange juice." He then asks, "How come you don't get apple juice?" And the answer is: "Because that is not what's inside." If you don't feel lovable, it is very hard to love others. You may try, but you will ultimately feel empty and sad because you don't treat yourself with the same love. You know the expression, *"Hurt people hurt people?"* That is what our minds are doing. Somewhere along the line, you got hurt—you got messages that you are not enough, and your mind wants to remind you of that all the time because it is hurt. We tell children (and adults, for that matter) not to bully each other. There are now anti-bullying laws that have been upheld in many states, with real consequences for the bully. So why do we do it to ourselves all day every day? I'll say it again, this makes no sense. And this stream of self-generated negative messages does so much damage.

There is a big difference between loving yourself, being self-centered, and feeling like you are better than others. I love myself and think I am a good person, but I do not feel like I am better than anyone else. **I do not love myself in comparison to others.** I love myself for who I am, as I am. And I am not perfect either. There are times I get down on myself or criticize myself or hear my own inner **Bully**. However, I am aware of this voice and when it talks, I do something about it. I don't allow it to drone on and on and be mean to me.

And I'm also able to look at myself and listen to others with whom I'm in a relationship. I know I am not perfect. I know I make mistakes. And then I look inside and see where I can grow and learn and get better. What I don't do is beat myself up over it and say mean, horrible things to myself. Would you parent a child that way? If your child or little cousin or anyone you love made a mistake, would you bully them and beat them down with all the ways they are horrible? I would hope not. And if you are reading this and thinking, "Yes, I might do that," then go back to the Wayne Dyer philosophy of "you can't give what you don't have inside." If that is all you have inside you, then that is probably why you would go about life that way.

Now it is time to have a relationship with the inner voice of your Best Friend. I know at first it might be hard and uncomfortable to listen to her. However, listening to the Bully is nothing more than an old habit. Remember the neuroplasticity we talked about in previous chapters? We are rewiring your brain to operate in a healthier manner. In the exercises in Scarlett's next chapter, you'll see how to practice listening to the voice of the Best Friend, instead of the Bully.

PART 2

Scarlett

GOING DEEPER AND PUTTING
HOW TO LIVE BY THIS NEW TRUTH
INTO PRACTICE

WHAT YOU THINK ABOUT GROWS

THIS CHAPTER IS FOCUSED on noticing our inner dialogue. We talk to ourselves all day long! What are we saying? When we notice the language we use and the attitude and tone we take to talk to ourselves, we can then recognize why we have limitations. We can examine the circumstances we are struggling with and identify the emotion that preceded these situations. Then we can back up one more step to the thought or belief that came first. It's taking a backward look at what we learned earlier:

Thoughts affect our emotions.
Emotions influence the choices we make.
Our choices directly shape our circumstances.

If we don't like our circumstances, whether it's a relationship, our living situation, or our career, we can think back to the emotion that influenced the choice we are living with now. Then we can think back to the limiting thoughts and beliefs that preceded the emotion.

So, what thoughts does our mind tend to focus on—what do we repeat to ourselves? Do we tell ourselves positive, nourishing, encouraging thoughts or low, heavy, pessimistic thoughts? Once we know our inner voice, we can train that voice to speak a different language.

This is another way we create the map that will take us where we want to go.

What do you think about yourself? What is the tone of your inner dialogue? Critical or Kind? **Best Friend** or **Bully?** Does it work to bully yourself? Why do bullies bully? What are they hiding about themselves behind the aggression and bravado?

Remember, the limbic brain over-amplifies danger to keep us safe from harm, ridicule, embarrassment, and failure. This becomes our inner critic or bully. It keeps us hidden and sheltered from others' opinions and judgments; this voice wants to keep us safe from feeling vulnerable.

Do you have to bully yourself? Do you have a choice about how you treat yourself?

What if you become your own best friend? How would that feel? What would change in your life? What would you have to give up? How does bullying yourself benefit or serve you in any way? Does your bully voice keep you protected and safe?

Let's do an experiment. For a whole day, notice your inner critic and shift the dialogue from bully to best friend. This is just an experiment; you can go back to the bully tomorrow if you want to. But notice what feelings come up. Write down what you notice with as much detail as you can.

I had a client named Jon. He was very successful, but always had a nagging fear that something was going to happen to take all his success away. When we investigated his inner dialogue and its origination, he remembered that when he was a child, his father had an ashtray that said, "If it wasn't for bad luck, I'd have no luck at all." He remembered his father was always waiting for "the other shoe to drop." This had a strong impact on Jon when he was young, and he seemed to always expect something bad to happen, even when good was happening. Once we knew where the source of the belief was coming from, Jon was liberated from it. He was able to recognize the thought pattern and change his dialogue, taking charge of the critic. We connected with the many experiences he had that were successful without "the other shoe dropping." We changed his inner dialogue to one of support, encouragement, and friendship. With that shift, he could allow his inner child that he had carried into his adult life to grow up.

Bully vs. **Best Friend** is a process developed by Phoenix.

PROCESS
BULLY VS. BEST FRIEND

One way I like to start this exercise is by naming the **Bully** and **Best Friend.** The bully could be any name. I have a client that named hers Jack, short for Jack Ass. Then think of a name that you love or makes you feel good. Now throughout your day, notice how you are feeling. If you are feeling down or bad, check in and see who is talking. Is it the **Bully** or the **Best Friend?** If it is the **Bully**, you can gently ask the **Best Friend** to speak up as well. I know this sounds hard because you might be thinking, "But how do I do that? I really do believe I am stupid or ugly, so I don't even know what the **Best Friend** would say."

That is an excellent question. First, I would try and write down the main themes of your negative beliefs. Then I would go through the Post It Note exercise in this book with each one. Once you have your Truth, your **Best Friend** can simply remind you of that. In the Post-It note exercise, we give examples of how this is done. So, if you have gone through the exercise using the very familiar and popular "I am so ugly" belief, and you realize that Beauty is subjective and we may not know what is beautiful and what is not, we can listen to the **Best Friend** as she might say something like, "Beauty is so subjective. I am choosing to believe that we are all beautiful and there are many versions of beauty. I am choosing to believe that my version is just as beautiful as the rest."

What is good about this is that you can have that response written down somewhere so each time the **Bully** wants to say you are ugly, you can listen to the **Best Friend** right away. And that is the voice you want to energize. There is a great app called Yapp-Gently Random Reminders. This app lets you program different messages you want to remember throughout your day. Then it will randomly remind you at different points throughout your day, keeping you in the flow of the expansive thoughts you are creating. What we focus on grows. Water the flowers, not the weeds as we have already talked about. Another good way to look at the voices is to ask yourself, "Would I want a roommate that talks to me the way the **Bully** talks to me?" I have asked that question to hundreds of people and 100% of the answers are "NO WAY."

Notice who is talking. And then decide what you want to feel in your life. And then listen to the voice that will get you where you want to feel. If we want to feel more confident, happier, calmer, and loving, then the **Best Friend** is the way to go. If we want to feel anxious, insecure, depressed, and unworthy, the **Bully** is the way to go. It is simple, but not easy. It is developing a new habit.

The choice is yours.

PROCESS
RELEASING THE LIMITATION

See yourself as a child who is hearing and seeing any limiting message and believing this old story. Speak to your child self from the place of an adult, as if you are your own healthy, healed parent. What would you say to comfort and soothe, give strength and confidence? Release the old, conditioned belief or fear into the earth, then step away from the spot it was released into. See yourself separate from it. You no longer need to carry this burden. You are free.

Create a new story around being your best friend. Visualize how you would talk to yourself. Feel it; see the child accepting and living your new story and then growing up to your current age.

Come back to the present time and journal about the new dialogue you are choosing.

PROCESS
CELEBRATE WHO YOU ARE RIGHT NOW

We often get so focused on what we want to achieve or where we want to be that we overlook where we are.

In this exercise, we practice mindfulness by pausing and acknowledging all the strengths, qualities, and achievements in this moment of our lives, and how we can use what we have to help us move forward and resolve any areas of struggle we have.

Begin by writing all you like about yourself and your life. What are your strengths and qualities; what have you come through and achieved? Make a list of everything big and small.

When you are finished, close your eyes, and allow all the good feelings to move through your body, emotions, and mind. Acknowledge, claim, and celebrate all that you are and all you've done. "I did this! I'm proud of myself. I see how powerful I am."

Now, take a separate paper or a page in your notebook and describe areas where you may be struggling. Next to each struggle, write one of your strengths or an example of one of your successes you can use to address this current struggle. Take a moment to write how you will use your previous—and current—accomplishments to overcome or work through any challenges you are tackling now.

This exercise emphasizes the strengths and abilities we already have and enables us to feel empowered and capable. We can step out of feeling like a victim or hopeless when we remember the power we already possess.

This exercise can also help us to feel useful in helping others who are struggling by offering our experience and strengths.

CHAPTER 8

Evoke the Rebel! Stay Strong!

"*I simply don't have it in me to define my life's success playing someone else's game and following someone else's rulebook.*"
—Dipa to her Grandfather

—DIPA SANATANI

Scarlett

IN THIS FINAL CHAPTER, we are going to learn how to play hardball with our thoughts! We have to get tough and determined with our own mind. This is where discipline comes into play. Our mind is accustomed to running the show. We have given it free rein and it has dragged us wherever it wanted. Every emotion we felt trapped by; all the discouraging and critical thoughts that have kept us feeling inadequate, small, and fearful have been the result of our thoughts and conditioned stories. Now is the time to take charge! So put on your leather jacket, get on the motorcycle of your mind, and change direction!

Thoughts influence the way we feel.
Feelings affect the choices we make.
Our choices become the conditions of our lives.

When we feel good, strong, and confident, we make very different choices than when we feel sad, insecure, and discouraged. Before making important decisions, work on shifting the tone and content of your thoughts to get the result you want.

An important piece of *Evoking the Rebel* is keeping your guard up. Learn to stand guard when it comes to your mind. Take charge of what you allow in and what you allow to happen inside your head. Imagine protecting your thoughts as if you are in a battle. You are on high alert for danger; but unlike the limbic brain, the dangers you are watching for are the negative, discouraging, thoughts that keep you trapped on a life path that is suffocating your joy, your juice, your passion, and your fulfillment.

Once you notice your brain is going down that path, *you*, the thinker, the one in charge, have to say *NO!* This is where we use our newly acquired practices to support us as we continue to build new neural pathways. In time, this becomes our natural thought process, and we no longer have to be on such high alert. We build resilience and strength, and the shift in thoughts happens more quickly and more easily.

Remember, no one can tell you what to think or feel. That's up to you to decide and control.

Making this change requires the courage to challenge the messages you're hearing and believing. *You have to dare to believe there is something more that is possible for your life.*

Where do you get the courage from? How do you stand up to the thoughts that have been running your life?

We ask the questions:

- Why do I want and need to make these changes in my life?
- Why would I want to change the limiting thoughts?
- What will I gain from it?
- How would that influence the way I feel and show up in my life?
- What will my life look like a year, or five years, from now if I keep the beliefs I hold now?

You can live a mediocre life, that's easy. Look around you, you'll see that everywhere. People just skimming by, making excuses for why they can't succeed, blaming everything and everyone around them for their unhappiness.

Living an extraordinary life takes courage and making and keeping a commitment to your best life to give you the strength and discipline to keep going when you want to just give in to comfortable and predictable patterns.

You also need a strong support system. You need people who will encourage and build you up when you feel discouraged and weak. Friends, teachers, and family who believe in you and know your commitment are essential to help you through these times.

Write a list of people you can rely on to help you and support you in staying connected to your vision and yearning.

Now you're ready to *Evoke the Rebel*!

MEDITATION
EVOKE THE REBEL

This is a guided journey to *Evoke your Rebel* who says *NO* to mediocrity. Our commitment is the Rebel's power to reject all the things inside ourselves keeping us small and limited and encourages us to rebel against our inner critic, our inner bully, our inner helpless victim, our laziness, or our inner blamer. Acknowledge your excuses and make the courageous stance to say *No* and remind yourself that you are in charge.

Begin with journeying to your **Sanctuary**. Spend a few moments relaxing here and disconnecting from the outside world. Drop into your inner realm.

As you explore your landscape, you notice a person up ahead. As you come closer, you can see it's your Inner Rebel. This is a version of yourself that you need to stay strong and connected to your vision. Using all of your senses, get to know this aspect of yourself. What do you look like as the Rebel? What are you wearing? What are your beliefs and convictions about yourself and your life's possibilities? Imagine the strength and power of *NO* emanating from your Rebel self as you fight and reject the conditioning of your old patterns.

Does your Rebel have a name? Spend some time getting to know your Rebel self; ask for advice and guidance on how to stay strong and connected to this part of yourself.

When you feel complete, make your way across your landscape with your Rebel self. Feel bigger, stronger, and more powerful than before you met her. Know she is always inside of you, an integral part of who you are that you can access whenever you need it.

As you complete this journey, visualize yourself feeling strong and victorious.

PROCESS
STAYING STRONG!

This is our final piece: How to stay connected to the work of reshaping our lives, one thought at a time!

Recognize and acknowledge what has worked for you. Where have you had the most success from this work? Where have you seen shifts in your life? What has been affected by this new work you've been doing? Look at your relationship with yourself first; then with those around you: peers, family, friends, and co-workers. What has shifted?

Write down in depth what you noticed, gained, and felt. Write your successes and what has contributed to these successful outcomes.

This is your map and your compass to keep you moving in the direction of your best life. When you feel yourself getting off track or feeling discouraged, read this. It will energize and stimulate what you know has *undeniably* worked for you. This keeps you accountable as well as strengthened to pick yourself up and move forward with compassion and power. This next process trains the brain where to focus and what to do with the power of that focus.

PROCESS
CELEBRATE ALL THAT YOU ARE!

Here, we're taking some time to acknowledge and celebrate our successes, large and small. For some, getting out of bed and dressed is a cause for celebration. We acknowledge that being *"here"* is a challenge, that figuring out how to move through this world to find your place in society and your family dynamic, plus all the physical changes and social pressures, takes a great deal of physical and mental energy and skill. Consider each of these elements as each success is celebrated. We all yearn to feel we are doing a good job in our lives, to have someone who is proud of us and impressed with who we are and what we've done.

In this exercise, we are going to become that person for ourselves. We are throwing a party for all we are and all we do. Why not? Who said we always have to bully ourselves and focus on our *"failures?"* This is one way to shift out of conditioned habits that keep us feeling small. Here, we continue to take charge of ourselves in a powerful, strong way.

- Take a few deep breaths, guiding the body and mind to relax. Give yourself a few moments to step out of your regular day to be here for yourself.
- As your body gets heavy and relaxed and your mind slows down, settle into your heart center. Connect with the beating of your own heart. Can you feel it? Say to yourself, "This is me." Take a moment to sink deeper. Connect with the space deep within yourself. Imagine your heart is opening up a beautiful space for you, a space welcoming you, where you feel excited and happy and safe.
- As you explore this space, see a big comfy chair just for you and a movie screen in front of it. Next to it is a table

with all your favorite snacks and drinks. The movie is a projection of your memories and positive thoughts about yourself. You can start with how you got up this morning and got ready for the day. Watch that on the screen with an attitude of appreciation. Then just allow all the memories to flow. They can be minor or momentous. A time you helped others, strangers, or peers; a kindness you extended to someone; a caring word, a smile you shared. Spend some time acknowledging all the things you may normally just pass over in a day.

When you feel complete, notice how it feels to acknowledge and celebrate yourself. You can imagine having a party and the people you love gathering around you to celebrate you. Create some affirmations.

I celebrate and respect all the good in my life.
I acknowledge and honor all the good within myself.

Connect with a feeling of happiness and excitement about your life and who you are.

Coming back to the heart center, allow all these memories and feelings to melt into your body and mind. Take a deep breath and repeat your mantra to yourself a few times before opening your eyes.

This can start a daily practice of self-celebration. At bedtime, do a review of the good you experienced, the good you shared or offered, big gestures and small, and give yourself some appreciation. Fall asleep with your positive, appreciative affirmations in your mind. Celebrate who you are, because, *Why Not?!*

Continue to use these tools to deepen your experiences. Claim them as your own. This is your life's toolbox.

Congratulations! You NOW have what you need to take charge first of your inner world, then of your outer world.

Remember, big change starts one thought at a time.

Conclusion

"I know where I'm going and I know the truth, and I don't have to be what you want me to be. I'm free to be what I want"

—MUHAMMAD ALI

Phoenix

Congratulations! You have made it through the book, completing each and every exercise—and *Voila!* You are now a calm, happy, positive, life-loving human!

Well, much as we wish it were instantly so, as we all know, it takes commitment and practice every day to change the mind and its habits. You have learned that the way we think and those thoughts we find circling round and round in our mind—chattering away their messages—are mostly a product of conditioning and habit. And the good news—you now have the skills and tools you need to be free of that conditioning and be that calm, happy, positive, life-loving person you truly are! It is just a matter of continued vigilance and practice.

In the last chapter, *Evoking the Rebel*, we discussed standing guard at the entrance to your mind. This is the key to everything. We will leave you with two more images you can conjure up when you are putting this into practice.

Imagine your mind is your house. For most of us, we have a front door that locks. Not only do we have a lock, but because many of us want to keep out burglars and strangers, we install an additional deadbolt lock, plus an alarm system to warn us if anyone tries to get past those locks, a video camera to check out whoever is outside, so we can decide if we will let them in, and we might also be part of a neighborhood watch where we keep an eye out for our neighbor's homes and yards and warn them if anyone or anything is threatening in the vicinity. Whew! We are careful!

But do we do the same for our minds?

Imagine having a thought and treating it like someone coming to your front door. Is this a thought you want to let in? If you let this thought in, what will it do to your house? A negative person will come into your home and go on and on about how awful everything is; they might even make a big mess in your home, and then what? You are left feeling crappy with a messy home.

Don't allow negative thoughts into your mind! Think of this as looking into your inner video camera and deciding what thoughts you want to let in. And if the alarm starts to ring—as in, feeling anxious, depressed, or hopeless—it might be time to check out those thoughts and decide if they should be let in at all!

And look out for one another. If you notice a friend or family member is feeling down or anxious, ask them to check their thoughts—much like you would with a neighborhood watch. Let's help each other out and look out for each other's mental health when possible. When a thought comes knocking, remember, **ask who it is and decide if that thought is welcome in your home!**

Here is one last image before we send you on your way. Imagine your thoughts are like little lamps. Lamps just sit there until we plug them in, and the bulbs light up. Imagine your thoughts are lamps. You know they are there; however, you must plug them in to energize them. Decide which thoughts you want to plugin. What are you choosing to energize? Are you plugging in anxious thoughts? If so, you are choosing to light up and energize anxiety. However, you have now learned that it is possible to simply notice the anxious thoughts without plugging them in. Just observe these thoughts, and then choose to plug in and energize a courageous *"light"* (thought!) instead. If you are going to light up your mind, wouldn't you rather light it up with lamps that feel good? That is the house I want to live in.

The choice is yours. It always was; it just takes using your new tools—awareness and practice.

You have now learned how to have that awareness. It's time to get out there and practice!!!!

About the Authors

Scarlett Denise Rizvi is a Soul-Full Life and Relationship coach. She leads workshops on mind mastery, meditation, and deep healing. Scarlett is the founder of From Wounds to Wisdom, which offers facilitator training for those seeking to deepen their personal healing practice as well as professionals who can offer this work to their clients. Scarlett lives in sunny Mexico with her husband, daughter, cat, and dog.

Phoenix Crosby is a Licensed Clinical Social Worker with over 20 years of experience working with individuals, families, and groups. She believes we have all the answers inside us and ultimately are our best guides to connect us to ourselves, enabling us to heal and trust our own inner wisdom. She has a private practice in addition to running workshops and trainings. Phoenix lives in New Jersey with her husband, two rescued dogs, and cat and loves spending time with her family, friends, and her new granddaughter Noelle.

Made in the USA
Middletown, DE
09 July 2023